The Village Blacksmith

Shoeing a fine Grey Percheron at the smithy at Chipping Hill, Essex. The three-footed iron stand is used for resting the horse's leg when a fore hoof is being shod

THE VILLAGE
BLACKSMITH

Ronald Webber

David & Charles : Newton Abbot

ISBN 07153 5363 2

To
the memory of
my father

By the same author
The Early Horticulturists 1968
Covent Garden: Mud Salad Market 1969

Type set by Bristol Typesetting Company
in Linotype Plantin
and printed in Great Britain
by Redwood Press Limited Trowbridge
for David & Charles (Publishers) Limited
South Devon House Newton Abbot Devon

Contents

Illustrations

ILLUSTRATIONS

Photographs not acknowledged above are from the author's collection

Preface

The village blacksmith as a worker in iron and a shoer of horses with his own 'shop' in the centre of a village has almost gone. The place that was once filled with the noise of horses and hammering and with the acrid smell of burning hoofs, and was the gossip mart of the area, has fallen before the onslaught of the motor age.

Some blacksmiths' shops have become garages, others workshops for artistic ironwork, but most have gone altogether, with a house name like *The Old Forge* the only reminder that here once was a thriving business.

In the blacksmiths' shops that remain, few of the occupants would dream of working so hard and for so long as the old village blacksmith was forced to do in order to earn a living. As Longfellow put it, his was a life of 'toiling, rejoicing, sorrowing', with no respite as old age made the heavy work harder and harder to manage.

In this book I have written of the village blacksmith who was a central figure of the community, a man not only blacksmith and farrier, but, at times, wheelwright, carpenter, tinker, veterinary surgeon, doctor, dentist, sportsman and many other things.

The term 'blacksmith' I have used in most instances to stand for 'farrier' as well. The Oxford English Dictionary describes 'blacksmith' as 'a smith who works in iron or blackmetal'. 'Farrier' it gives as 'shoeing smith', from the Old French *ferrier* and the Latin *ferrarius,* or from *ferrum* meaning iron. A farrier was also the man who had charge of the horses in a cavalry regiment, where he had a title such as farrier-major or sergeant-farrier. But as far as the village blacksmith was concerned he was generally both smith and farrier.

I refer to the workshop of the smith at various times as the smithy, forge, or blacksmith's shop, all of which names are in common usage.

1

The Worker in Iron

'For Anncesterie of tyme oh! who canne tell
The first beginning of so old a trade'
                    Robert Glover: *Ode* of 1612

The blacksmith, master craftsman throughout the centuries, came
into being with the discovery of iron as a workable metal some
2,500 to 3,000 years ago. At that period iron was being used
occasionally in Mesopotamia and Egypt, but it was the Hittites
of Asia Minor who first began to work it on a large commercial
scale and to trade it freely with their neighbours. From Asia
Minor it was brought to Europe where the Greeks popularised it
and in the fifth century BC it reached Britain, spelling the end
of the Bronze Age.

Not that iron—at least as first produced—was greatly superior
to bronze: it was only slightly harder and certainly not so
attractive in appearance. To begin with it was used only for
ornament. But it was plentiful, and once the smelting of it was
understood and furnaces could be brought to a sufficient heat it
could be produced much more cheaply than bronze, with the
result that good tools and weapons could be provided for the

many rather than for the select few.

The first users of iron—the pioneer blacksmiths—were no doubt held somewhat in awe by the ordinary man. The metal was new and the blacksmiths were astute enough to keep the secrets of working it very much to themselves. It was extremely malleable when heated red hot, and it could be heated and forged and re-heated and re-forged until the exact shape of the required tool or weapon had been achieved. And the fact that the smith had made fire his servant added to his reputation.

The coming of iron was the starting-point of some very important developments in Britain. The iron axes of the Celts and later of the Belgae brought the forests of the plains under cultivation and the heavy iron-tipped plough went deeply into the soil and turned it over. The farmers extended the areas under their control and intensified their methods of agriculture. The Saxons carried this progress still further with forest reclamation and the tillage of the stiffer soils of the valleys.

It was the blacksmith who made all this possible and in these early ages he reigned supreme among craftsmen. Equipped with a forge, a hearth fired by charcoal or other suitable fuel, an anvil, a hammer and tongs, he must have been an impressive figure, and he was able to produce and repair almost all the things needed for agriculture, domestic life and war. In *Evangeline* Longfellow spoke of him with great regard:

> *For, since the birth of time, throughout all ages and nations,*
> *Has the craft of the smith been held in repute by the people.*

Not everyone in the early days liked iron. Hesiod the Greek, in whose time it was something new, thought it evil. Herodotus also said it brought harm to mankind. Ovid maintained that the earth hid the iron because it was bad and that when it was brought out by man it caused destruction and horror. Centuries later, Mahomet recognised it had a duality: when used for peaceful purposes it could bring many advantages; but when applied to increase the size and scope of war it was an instrument of evil.

It is probable that horse-shoeing, as we know it today, did not begin until about the ninth century AD, for before the days of artificial roads shoes were not essential. The Greeks had what they called a hippo-sandal which was strapped to the horse's foot, but it seems likely that this was merely to hobble the horse and not to protect its feet while travelling. There is nothing to indicate that at that time iron shoes were used. On the Elgin Marbles from the Parthenon of Athens, which are in the British Museum, the horses are sculptured in great detail, but there are no signs of shoes. A silver coin of Traentum dated 360 BC shows a lad holding up the foot of a horse but no shoe is to be seen.

Nor is it thought that the Romans in Britain had shoes on their horses, though cavalry was used extensively towards the end of the Roman era. We do, however, know that a plate was sometimes tied to a damaged foot to prevent further injury. In those days before shoeing, riders would dismount and would lead their horses over rough, hard ground, and if the difficult terrain continued for some distance, a mule was often ridden and the horse led—for the feet of a mule are thicker and tougher than those of a horse.

Shoeing with an iron plate and nails, however, was known to some Celtic and Germanic tribes before the Roman conquest. Possibly the Druids were familiar with the art and acted as early blacksmiths to shoe the war or chariot horses but if so, it may be that they kept their method secret from the Romans. The ancient Britons were a horse-loving people and possessed many horses: Cassivelanus the British chieftain, who commanded all Britain against the Romans, is reported to have retained 4,000 war chariots around him after sending away all his other troops.

It is possible that King Arthur and his knights of the Round Table shod their horses, for at St Columb in Cornwall there is a large stone with deep marks on it which legend says were made by the hoofs of Arthur's horse. This dinting of the stone by the plunging animal is mentioned by Walter Scott in his poem *The Bridal of Triermain* where King Arthur is tempted by Gwendolen to drink from a goblet.

Not until the ninth century are horseshoes specifically mentioned. In a list of cavalry equipment issued by the Roman
Leo VI there is reference to 'lunar or crescent-shaped iron shoes
and their nails'.

With the coming of the iron horseshoe the blacksmith was
even more important and he became busier, for the shoeing of
warhorses and chariot horses was additional to his work as
weapon- and tool-maker and armourer. As the years went by
the various jobs became specialised and there arose blacksmiths, farriers and armourers. There was also the maréchal
(*mariscalcus, manesculcus, marescallus, mareschallus, mareschal*),
whose name was probably derived from Old Frankish *marhshelk,*
literally 'horse-servant'. A maréchal was a man who had charge
of the horses in Norman France. The Normans brought their
maréchals to England with them and the name soon became
anglicised to marshall. One line of marshalls became the Earls of
Pembroke and the seventh earl, Walter Marshall, who died in
1246 had on his seal a horseshoe and nails. The word maréchal
or marshall remained in vogue long after Norman French ceased
to be the court language; but it gradually gave way to ferrier,
ferrator, or farrier, derived from the Latin *faber ferrarius,* a man
who not only worked in iron but also shod horses. Maréchal in
France later became the title of the highest dignitary in the land:
an ordinary farrier is known as a *maréchal ferrant.*

At Bannockburn in 1318 William le Maréchal, Anselm le
Maréchal and Thomas de Ferrers were fighting on the English
side. About this time, too, a family called Ferrier lived at Tranent
in Scotland and had for its seal three horseshoes. The Ferrers
family of Tutbury in Staffordshire is said to stem from Henry
de Farrariis or Ferrers who was in charge of all the farriers
employed on William the Conqueror's horses. Six horseshoes are
included in the coat of arms of the Ferrers family.

William gave the town of Northampton and the hundred of
Falkley to one of his followers Simon St Liz on condition that

he provided shoes for the royal horses when the King was hunting in that area. Another follower, Henry de Averyng, held the manor of Norton in Essex

> in capite *of our Lord the King by the serjeantry of finding a manor with a horse, value ten shillings, and four horse-shoes, one sack of barley and one iron buckle, as often as it may happen that our Lord the King should go with his army into Wales at his proper expense for forty days.*

A Saxon chief Gamelhere was allowed to retain certain land at Welbeck in Nottinghamshire on condition that he shod the king's horses whenever the reigning monarch visited the Manor of Mansfield. It he did the job properly the king was obliged to present him with a palfrey worth four marks; but if he bungled the job and lamed a horse he had to replace it with one of his own.

By this time, the shoeing of horses and the working of iron were being given much attention, for shoeing had become very necessary now that the Normans and their horses were both wearing armour. A heavier shoe was introduced; those made by the Celts had been fastened by three nails on either side in countersunk holes which produced a bulge on either side of the shoe, but now the shoes became broader and flatter with no countersinking. This kind of shoe was to last until the end of the sixteenth century, which saw the introduction of the practice of fullering, ie punching a groove in which the nail holes are made.

In Norman times the draught horse was fairly rare, for the state of the roads did not generally allow the passage of wheeled vehicles. The war horse was kept for state occasions or for battles, while the hobelar, a light cavalry horse, was used for quick travelling, hawking and similar sports. The court travelled on horseback.

Hunting was popular and even the clergy took part in this sport. When the Archdeacon of Richmond arrived at Bridling-

ton in 1216 he brought ninety-seven horses with him. In 1256 the
Bishop of Norwich bequeathed his pack of hounds to Henry III.
The Abbot of Tavistock, who had a pack of hounds, was ordered
by his bishop to break it up. The Abbot of Leicester had so good
a stud of hunters that the king paid him an annual fee so that he,
the king, might come with his friends to hunt with the abbot.
Wycliffe in the next century was to speak out against the priests
who had 'fair horses and jolly gay saddles and bridles ringing
by the way'.

Shoeing a horse in a frame in the fourteenth century. From a manuscript in
the Bodleian Library

Although the Normans considered the shoeing of horses important, it was still not always accepted as necessary by other
people. In his *Norman Horseshoe* Sir Walter Scott writes of a
battle on the banks of the Rynny between the forces led by the
Norman Marcher lords and the Welshmen of Glamorgan. The
unshod Welsh horses were inferior to the heavy iron-shod
chargers of the Normans, but their footing was surer and this
won the day for the Welshmen.

William the Conquerer himself may have lost his life through
riding a shod horse. One story is that he was hunting when his

Woodcut of a blacksmith from William Caxton's *Game and Play of the Chess,* 1483

horse slipped and threw him, and it is possible that if the horse had not been shod it would not have slipped.

The first smithies began to appear about the thirteenth century and these early ones were open on four sides with just a roof. In 1235 Walter le Bruin, farrier or maréchal, had a piece of land granted to him in the Strand by Henry III, on which he was given permission to put up a forge on condition that he should pay a yearly quit-rent of 'six horse-shoes with the nails thereto belonging'.

Under the feudal system of medieval times the country blacksmith was a servant of the manor like most other people. He burnt charcoal obtained from his lord's forests, dined in hall when the lord was in residence and being a landowner as well as a smith, had his land ploughed by the lord's ploughs.

At Amberley in Sussex, Benet Smith held four acres belonging to the smithy on the Bishop of Chichester's manor and his services included having to mind all the iron 'gear' belonging to two of the bishop's ploughs and to shoe two horses 'plus the serjeant's horse'. He also had to grind the scythes used in the bishop's meadows and all the shears.

The blacksmith was a man of some substance in the community. Besides being occupied on the business of the manor he worked for the village builder and repaired waggons, carts and ploughs for the farmers. He tyred wheels and made and repaired farm implements. He made his own tools and had his own grindstone.

Such a man of importance would have been the smith Gervase of Chaucer's *Miller's Tale*, to whom Absalon the love-sick parish clerk went for a red-hot coulter with which to have his revenge on Alison and Nicholas. Gervase

> . . . *in his forge smithed plough-harneys*
> *He sharpeth shaer and coulter busily.*

Blacksmithing and horseshoes have left their mark in many places of Britain. Hammersmith, probably a compound of Old English Hamor and Smyththe, was known as Hamersmyth as early as 1294.

John of Gaunt is said to have ridden into Lancaster where his horse threw a shoe. The townspeople took the shoe and preserved it.

The coat of arms of the county of Rutland has a horseshoe as the central feature, and there is an ancient custom of the Rutland county town of Oakham by which

> *the first time any Peer of this Kingdom shall pass through*
> *the precincts of his Lordship, he shall forfeit as a Homage*

Coat of arms of the county of Rutland,
with downward pointing horseshoes

*a Shoe from the Horse whereon he rideth, unless he redeem
it with money.*

Henry I seems to have made a grant of the Manor of Oakham
to Henry de Ferrers, who held it from 1131 to his death in 1156.
He was succeeded by his son Walkelin, who probably built Oakham Castle, part of which stands today as probably the most
perfect remaining piece of domestic architecture of the twelfth
century in England.

The horseshoes contributed by peers passing through the town
were originally nailed to the gate of Oakham Castle, but today
they are kept hanging on an old board inside the hall of the
castle. This strange tax in the shape of a horseshoe, or money in
lieu, was one of the ways in which de Ferrers showed his power
as Lord of the Manor, but it was also a means of collecting
what must have been quite a substantial amount of money—for
most people no doubt preferred to pay up rather than part with
a shoe.

At Dover in Kent there was at one time a somewhat similar
custom. The Mayor took a toll of a halfpenny for every horse
travelling through the town, and the money was used for the
repair of the harbour.

There is another version of the Oakham custom which says

that Elizabeth I when passing through the town found her horse
lame from the loss of a shoe and tried in vain to find a blacksmith. Peeved at this, she issued a royal edict to the effect that
every peer of the realm should either forfeit a horseshoe when
riding through Oakham or pay a fine. But the custom appears to
have started long before the time of Queen Elizabeth.

Among the shoes which hang in Oakham Castle there are many
royal ones. The label of one of them claims that it was presented
by Queen Elizabeth I, but there seems to be some doubt about
the truth of this. But the second Queen Elizabeth certainly gave
a horseshoe when she visited the castle in 1967, and she is said to
have supervised personally the design and making of it. Other
royal shoes to be seen there include those presented by Queen
Victoria, Edward VII, George VI, the Duke of Windsor, and
Prince Philip, Duke of Edinburgh. The ancient custom still goes
on, with the result that there are no fewer than 218 shoes now
exhibited in the castle. The rank of the donor peer is shown
by the form of coronet which surmounts the shoe.

Over the doorway leading to the Magistrates Court in Oakham
Castle is a small gilt horseshoe known as the Golden Shoe. This
was given by Lord Willoughby d'Eresby in 1840 after it had been
taken off his favourite horse Clinker. About 1843 it disappeared
and was given up for lost. Fifteen years later, however, it was
returned by the rector of a country parish, who confessed that
when he had been a scholar in Oakham, he, with two or three
other boys, had entered the castle and taken away the shoe.

Gloucester, being close to the Forest of Dean where iron mines were worked by the Romans and early Britons, was always a town of blacksmiths and the Via Fabrorum of Roman Gloucester still retains the name of Long Smith Street. Prince Rupert set up his smithy somewhere in Gloucester during the siege of 1643. Alcester in Warwickshire was also from an early period noted for its smiths and forges. Beverley Minster has a misericord showing a man shoeing a goose which is thought to date from about 1400.

In 1616 the English ambassador to the court of France took into Paris a horse shod with silver shoes which had deliberately been nailed on only lightly. When the ambassador came before a group of high French officials he caused the horse to prance vigorously so that the shoes flew off; they were caught by the officials and kept as souvenirs.

The pattern of horseshoes varied in different countries and in different parts of the same one, and an expert blacksmith was able to tell from which part of his country a shoe came. When Charles I fled to Dorset after the battle of Worcester to get a boat to France he pretended to be a groom. But when he stopped at a forge on the south coast to have a cast shoe dealt with, the blacksmith said to him, 'What manner of man are you whose horse has been shod in three different counties and one of them Worcestershire?'

Fugitives on various occasions were said to have reversed the shoes on their horses in the hope that their pursuers would think they were going in the opposite direction. In a museum in Hull there is a small strange shoe said to have been used by Mary Queen of Scots for this purpose. But experts think that it is far more likely to be a surgical shoe for a horse with strained tendons, and in any case it is unsuitable for general road work. Robert the Bruce is also said to have used the reversed-shoe method of escaping from his pursuers, as did Sir Walter Tyrrell when he was fleeing after having killed King William Rufus in the New Forest.

Opposite: Seventeenth-century blacksmith. The coat of arms is a simplified version of that of the Worshipful Company of Blacksmiths, shown on page 36. From *A Merry New Ballad both Pleasante and Sweet*, about 1661

German
fifteenth century

Spanish
twelfth century

English
fourteenth century

North African
twelfth century

German shoe of
the Crusades

French shoe of
the Crusades

Roman
first century

Arabian Morhest
early twentieth
century

Circassian
twelfth century

Spanish
nineteenth century

German
thirteenth century

Hunnish
sixteenth century

Chinese
early twentieth
century

Horseshoes of different countries. From the *Farriers' Annual*, 1911

Iron anvils do not appear to have been made much until the end of the sixteenth century; probably stout blocks of wood or lumps of iron ore were used instead. In 1586 Sir Edward Stradling refers to an anvil which had been hired out by Robert Hensley of Scoarthy, Somerset, to Thomas Sulley of St Athan, Glamorgan for the term of one year at a rent of 3s 4d.

Horseshoes appear in many inn signs, an indication of the importance of the blacksmith and his work in the community. *The Three Horseshoes* is quite a common one and others include the *Horse and Horse Shoe, Sun and Horse Shoe, Magpie and Horse Shoe, Horns and Horse Shoe,* and *Hoop and Horse Shoe.* There are also many *Farrier's Arms* and *Blacksmith's Arms.* There is an inn at Godmanstone in Dorset, the *Smith's Arms,* which is said to be the smallest inn in the country and which was originally a blacksmith's shop. According to legend King Charles II stopped there to have his horse shod and asked for a drink, to which the smith replied that he had no licence. The king thereupon granted him a licence and it has been in existence for over 300 years, though the blacksmith's business was discontinued long ago.

Like all tradesmen the blacksmith had his patron saint, St Eloi (Eloy, Lo, Loo, Laudus, Eligius, Loy or Loye) being shared by blacksmiths and other metal workers.

> And Loye the smith doth looke to horse, and smithies of
>   all degree;
> If they with iron meddle here, or if they goldsmithes be.
>   (Barnaby Googe: *Popish Kingdome*)

Eloi, born at Chaptelat near Limoges in AD 588, was the son of an artisan, Eucherius, and became apprentice to the goldsmith Abbo who was master of the Mint at Limoges. After serving his apprenticeship he crossed the Loire to Paris where he worked for Bobbo, treasurer to Clotaire II. Here, among other things, he made two thrones for the king and ended up as master of the Mint. He is described as 'tall, with a fresh complexion, his

hair and his beard curling without artifice; his hands shapely and
long-fingered, his face full of angelic kindness and its expression
grave and unaffected'.

After Clotaire's death the new king Dagobert gave Eloi an
estate at Solignai in Limousin in which to found a monastery.
The monastery that Eloi established followed the combined rules
of St Columbus and St Benedict. Dagobert also gave Eloi a house
in Paris which he promptly turned into a nunnery. In 641 Eloi
was appointed bishop of Noyon. He died nineteen years later.

Eloi was, for a long time, one of the most popular saints
of France and during the later Middle Ages his feast on the first
day of December was kept throughout north-western Europe. He
was renowned for the making of thrones and other metal objects,
but his chief claim to fame as a blacksmith was a neat piece of
horse-shoeing.

The story goes that a horse possessed of a devil was brought to
him at his forge. It just would not stand still to be shod. Eloi,
without hesitation, cut off the horse's leg that needed shoeing,
nailed the shoe on to it, and then put the leg back on the stump,
using the sign of the Cross to make it unite quickly and effectively.

Another version is that he cut off all four legs and restored
them. A bystander tried to imitate him but only succeeded in
killing the horse, whereupon Eloi chided him and restored the
horse to life.

At Alderney in Brittany is a chapel to St Eloi in which he
is represented as shoeing a horse which has its right front foot
missing. When farmers passed this chapel they used to make their
horses bow their heads in respect.

Most representations of Eloi show him with a horse. At St
Michael's. Church, Highworth, in Wiltshire there is a mural
distemper picture, probably of the thirteenth or fourteenth
century, which shows a chapel-like building containing a forge
with a blazing fire, and bellows and a trough and tongs nearby.
Eloi, in full array of church vestments, stands behind a strange
anvil holding a hammer in his right hand. A horse is resting

St Eloi (seventh century), patron saint of blacksmiths and other metal workers, holds the horse's leg that he has cut off to shoe. From the Luttrell Psalter

its hoof on the anvil and Eloi is shoeing it. Watching him is the Devil.

Eloi dressed as a bishop and holding the leg of a horse appears in a sculptured panel in the church porch at Wincanton in Somerset. The church at Durweston in Dorset has a sculpture of Eloi over the south door. At Freckenham in Suffolk, a small fourteenth-century alabaster panel shows a blacksmith, hammer in hand, holding a horse's leg on to the anvil. The Dukes of Burgundy gave silver to the blacksmiths who shod their horses on St Eloi's Day. In Chaucer's Prologue to *The Canterbury Tales* his Nun's greatest oath was 'By Saint Loy!'

A move to discredit St Eloi, and to bring back the ancient Vulcan, was made at the time of the Reformation. Vulcan the

Roman god of fire, the Hephaestus of Greek mythology, was the great artisan of the universe and at his vast workshop in Olympus he fashioned armour for the warriors of the heroic age. On earth volcanoes were his forges and his favourite residence was at Lemnos in the Aegean Sea. Beneath Mount Etna, with the aid of the Cyclops, he forged the thunderbolts of Jove.

The Cyclops of ancient mythology were believed to have invented the art of forging, and the discovery of the peculiar properties of iron were attributed to certain mythical beings, the Dactyls, who lived in Phrygia and who were thought to have acquired their knowledge from observations of the fusion of metals at the fabulous burning of Mount Ida. The Dactyls had the reputation of being wizards whose very names, Celnius, Damnameneus and Acmon, possessed a mysterious protective power when pronounced by persons exposed to sudden dangers.

In the *Kalevalla*, an ancient epic Finnish poem, the blacksmith Ilmaainen is represented as the pioneer and most skilled of artisans who fashioned both the weapons of war and the domestic implements and utensils.

England's own saint who represents the blacksmiths is Dunstan. He was born in AD 910 near Glastonbury in Somerset and he belonged to a noble family closely allied to the ruling house. As a lad he was sent to the court of King Athelstan but he seems to have fallen out with some of its members, who managed to get him expelled for 'practising incantations'. And as he left they threw him into a cess-pool.

Dunstan went off at once to his uncle Alphege the Bald, Bishop of Winchester, later to be canonised, who advised him to embrace the religious life, in which, for one thing, he would be unlikely to suffer such indignities as had been imposed upon him at the king's court. Dunstan took a while to consider, but a sudden recovery from a skin disease (which he thought was leprosy) persuaded him that God really wanted him to do this.

He returned to Glastonbury and built himself a small cell next to the church. Here he spent his time in prayer, study and

Opposite: St Dunstan (tenth century), patron saint of British blacksmiths, punishes the Devil who has tempted him. From the Luttrell Psalter

manual labour. His labour took the form of making bells and sacred vessels for the church and of illuminating books. He is said to have made two bells for Abingdon church. He also played the harp.

Dunstan installed a small forge in his cell, and one night while he was working there, the whole neighbourhood was aroused by a terrible howling which came from the small building. Then the rock on which the cell was built split into three. The local people rushed to the cell expecting the worst. But Dunstan, unharmed and still working at his forge, told them calmly that he had been visited by Satan. The Devil had appeared in the form of a beautiful girl—but Dunstan had not been deceived. He had taken up a pair of red hot tongs from his forge and had applied them to the girl's nose. The roar that came from her showed immediately that she was the Devil in disguise—no human could have howled like that!

Another version of the legend says that the incident took place at Mayfield in Sussex and that the Devil in his agony jumped from there to Tunbridge Wells, where he landed with a force so great that it caused a spring to flow. Yet another version has the Devil asking Dunstan to shoe him; but Dunstan recognises his customer, ties him to the wall and, in shoeing him, proceeds to cause him great pain and does not release him until he promises never again to enter a building where a horseshoe is displayed.

When King Athelstan died his brother Edmund, who succeeded him, persuaded Dunstan to return to court and made him Abbot of Glastonbury. Dunstan had very mixed fortunes during the

subsequent short reigns, at one time being driven into exile and living in Flanders, but towards the end of his life he was made Archbishop of Canterbury, and he remained in that office, a respected figure, until his death in 968. Since then, the tales of his temptation by the Devil together with his dexterity as a metal worker led many blacksmiths in England to consider Dunstan their patron saint, and his feast day is still celebrated.

Other blacksmiths have preferred Saint Clement as their representative. He had an anvil as an emblem and is said to have been martyred by being tied to an anchor and thrown into the sea.

The Day of St Clement, 23 November, was observed by blacksmiths as a day to be taken off work, and was often celebrated with loud explosions of gunpowder on anvils and a procession with an effigy of St Clement. This custom seems to have been particularly in vogue in government dockyards, but it was also followed in some private establishments where it was usual for the master to provide the wherewithal for a feast in the evening.

Old Clem, as he is familiarly called, was the chief figure in an annual ceremony by blacksmiths at Chatham and Woolwich dockyards as late as the nineteenth century. Hone's *Everyday Book* for 1826 gives an account of this celebration on the evening of St Clement's Day by the blacksmith apprentices of Woolwich. A senior apprentice, dressed up with cloak, wig and mask to represent Old Clem, was seated on a throne, and before him he had a wooden anvil, a pair of tongs and a hammer. His masked mate had a sledge hammer and there were several attendants. Old Clem opened the proceedings with a speech about his travels round the world and his arrival in London, where he had found all the 'gentlemen Vulcans' of Woolwich hard at work.

A procession with drum and fife, torches and banners then moved off round the town bearing Old Clem shoulder high and stopping for refreshments at all the inns on the way. They also called on the blacksmiths and officers of the dockyard, and at each stop Old Clem told his brief history of St Clement and money boxes were handed round.

The money they collected paid for the apprentices' supper, at which it was usual for the oldest to take the chair and the youngest the vice-chair. It was a merry occasion. The first toast was:

> Here's to old Vulcan, as bold as a lion,
> A large shop and no iron,
> A big hearth and no coal,
> And a large pair of bellowses full of holes.

And the second toast:

> True hearts and sound bottoms,
> Check shirts and leather aprons.

And finally:

> To the memory of Old Clem, and prosperity to all his descendants.

A 'Clem' supper was also held at the Bugle Inn, Twyford, Hampshire on St Clement's Day up to about 1880 and before that at the Dolphin. Here the toast of the evening was 'The Blacksmiths' and this was followed by the reading of the blacksmiths' legend of King Solomon. The story is recorded by the Hampshire Field Club in their *Proceedings*, and it tells how Solomon gave a feast for all the architects and artificers who had completed his splendid temple at Jerusalem. But he omitted to invite the blacksmith, or Son of the Forge, who came unbidden to the festal chamber, and, on Solomon's irate enquiry for his reasons, proved to the king that as he made all the tools which the other workers used he was indeed their superior and himself a master craftsman.

This story of who was the most important craftsman appears in several other forms. One says that it was King Alfred who, wishing to build a big palace, called together all the craftsmen and announced that the man doing the best work would be proclaimed 'Father of all craftsmen'. When the castle was finished the king

Twankydillo.

Which makes my bright ham_mer to rise and to fall, Here's to old Cole, and to young Cole, and to
old Cole of all, Twan-ky-dil-lo, twan-ky-dil-lo, twan-ky-dil-lo, dil-lo, dil-lo,
dil-lo, A roar-ing pair of bagpipes made of the green wil-low.

1. HERE'S a health to the jolly blacksmith, the best of all fellows,
   Who works at his anvil while the boy blows the bellows;
   Which makes my bright hammer to rise and to fall,
   Here's to old Cole,* and to young Cole, and to old Cole of all,
   Twankydillo,
   A roaring pair of bagpipes made of the green willow.

2. If a gentleman calls his horse for to shoe,
   He makes no denial of one pot or two,
   For it makes my bright hammer to rise and to fall,
   Here's to old Cole, and to young Cole, and to old Cole of all,
   Twankydillo,
   And he that loves strong beer is a hearty good fellow.

3. Here's a health to King Charlie and likewise his queen,
   And to all the royal little ones where'er they are seen;
   Which makes my bright hammer to rise and to fall,
   Here's to old Cole, and to young Cole, and to old Cole of all,
   Twankydillo,
   A roaring pair of bagpipes made of the green willow.

A very early Sussex folk song for blacksmiths. * Some versions had 'Clem',
'colt', 'foal' or 'goat' instead of 'Cole'

gave a big banquet which all the craftsmen attended, each bring-
ing a specimen of his work with the tools used in working it.
Everyone had done a good job, so to avoid jealousy King Alfred
gave the title to his tailor, who had made a coat of 'surpassing
beauty of colour and exquisite fashion'.

The blacksmith was angry at this and did not return to his
forge after the banquet, with the result that the mason could
not procure new tools, the carpenter could not get chisels, the
broken hinges of the gates could not be mended, the horses of
the king could not be shod, the tailor's broken scissors could
not be repaired, and the warriors could not fight properly
without weapons in good condition. So King Alfred and all the
craftsmen broke into the smithy and tried to do the work themselves. But they failed, and the scene in the smithy became one
of chaos and confusion, with the accidental breaking of the
anvil as the final catastrophe.

At this juncture who should walk in but St Clement with the
blacksmith beside him, the latter very angry at the wreckage of his
forge. St Clement said nothing but he seemed to enjoy the dis-
comfiture of the king and his company. At last the king, making
a humble bow to St Clement, said, 'I have made a great mistake
in allowing my judgement in this important matter to be governed
by the gaudy colour and stylish cut of the tailor's coat; and in
justice to the blacksmith, without whom none of us can do, I
proclaim him father of all the craftsmen.'

Then the king held another banquet at which the blacksmith
was guest of honour and obliged with a song, *Twankydillo,* which
has been handed down as a folk song. (The final line of the
chorus is a corruption of

> *a roaring pair of blowpipes* (ie bellows) *bound round with
> green willow*

for willow withes were bound round the leather at the nozzle of
the forge bellows to protect it from fire.)

The blacksmith's success, however, made the tailor spiteful and jealous. He crept under the table and snipped pieces out of the smith's apron—and that is why today the blacksmiths often have a fringe on their aprons.

Charles Dickens has a reference to Old Clem in *Great Expectations,* where Joe Gargery the blacksmith sings:

Hammer boys round—Old Clem!
With a thump and a sound—Old Clem!
Beat it out, beat it out—Old Clem!
With a clink for the stout—Old Clem!
Blow the fire, blow the fire—Old Clem!
Roaring dryer, soaring higher—Old Clem!

'It was not a very ceremonious way of rendering homage to a patron saint,' commented Dickens in *Great Expectations,* 'but I believe Old Clem stood in that relation towards smiths. It was a song that imitated the measure of beating upon iron, and was a mere lyrical excuse for the introduction of Old Clem's respected name.'

In the United States the legend of the blacksmith and King Solomon is well known from the picture entitled 'The Ironworker and King Solomon', which was painted by Christian Schussele as a commission from Joseph Harrison Jr of Philadelphia. Schussele was born in Alsace in 1824, studied in Paris, and settled in the United States in 1847 where for eleven years he was director of the Pennsylvania Art School. He died at Merchantville, N.Y. in 1879. The story of the commissioning of the picture is told in a little book *The Iron Worker and King Solomon* by Joseph Harrison Jr, printed in 1868 for private circulation. In it is a rendering of the legend in verse composed by Mr Harrison.

Other saints and holy men have been concerned with the trade of the blacksmith. St Martin, the patron saint of all who travel on horseback, has a horseshoe as an emblem. In the Middle Ages many a traveller when having his horse shod for a long and possibly dangerous journey would have an extra shoe made to hang at home to ensure the protection of Saint Martin.

Easterwine, Abbot of Wearmouth in the seventh century, is described by Bede as a strong humble man who 'when he went forth on the business of the monastery, if he found the brethren working, he would join them and work with them, by taking the plough handle, or handling the smith's hammer . . .'

Columbus, a holy man who lived in the centre of Ireland in the sixth century, was described as a *faber ferrarius*; St Columbus of Iona was a colleague.

St Egwin, who founded the monastery of Evesham, once went to Alcester in Warwickshire to preach to the smiths there, who were known to be very arrogant. As he preached they thumped their hammers on their anvils. So Egwin, 'full of love and mercy', prayed to God that the smiths would be destroyed—which they were, immediately!

2

The Worshipful Companies

'By hammer and hand all arts do stand'
Motto of the Guild of Blacksmiths, 1610

Strong individualist though he always was, the blacksmith found
it necessary, from very early days, to join with his fellow smiths
in the defence of the standards of their trade. In the thirteenth
century they were already beginning to become organised. When
a number of London citizens came before the Mayor in 1299 to
answer a charge of unlawful assembly they pleaded that they
had only met to discuss the regulation of the trade of smiths and
'to maintain a wax taper in honour of the Blessed Mary and St
Laudus (St Eloi)'.

Among the early ranks of blacksmiths were gunsmiths and
clockmakers but later each of these crafts formed an independent
organisation. Thomas Tompion, the eminent seventeenth-century
English clockmaker, is thought to have been a member of the
Guild of Blacksmiths.

The first grant of arms to this Guild was made by Sir Thomas
Holme, Clarenceux King of Arms in 1490. This patent no longer
exists, but its arms were: 'sable a cheveron silver betwene thre
hamorys crouned gold. The crest upon a healme a fenyx in his

Sixteenth-century blacksmith, from a Flemish woodcut. His tools were much the same as those of today

proper colours, a croune of gold about his necke with a chayne, stondinge upon a Tarege within a wreathe gold and sable'.

The first charter for the Guild of Blacksmiths came in 1571, and includes in its elaborate illuminated border a painting of the Company's arms which agrees with the 1490 description, except that the hammers are shown with silver heads.

In the *Liber Recordum* of 1575-6, a contemporary book of records, there is a proclamation by Queen Elizabeth I touching a Worcester blacksmith:

> *By the Queen—Right well beloved, we grete you well, and woll and comaund you to staye and noe further proceede in the suyte by you, Richard Porter, brought against Richard Bullock, before the bailiffs of our cittie of Worcester, for exercising the occupation or mysterie of a blacksmith for the space of one year nexte before the fyrst of May last past, not*

having been apprentice to the said occupation according to the tenour of the statutes in that case made and provyded, until the same matter be first harde and examined by our Council in our Marches of Wales; and for that entente, you, the said Richard Porter, do come and appear before our said Council ye fourth daye of November next, to answer on that p'tie (part) as shall appertayne, not failinge hereof upon payne of cli. Given under our signet at our town of Salopp, XXIV days of October, in ye XVI yere of our rayne.

A second charter was granted to the Guild by James I in 1605 and yet another by Charles I in 1639. A fresh patent of arms was granted in 1610 and was:

> *Sable a chevron or between three hammers argent handled and crowned or.*
> Crest: *On a wreath of the colours a phoenix proper standing upon a hill vert firing herself with the sun's beams.*
> Mantling: *Sable doubled or.*
> Motto: *By hammer and hand all arts do stand.*

Coat of arms of the Worshipful Company of Blacksmiths, showing three crowned hammers, 1610

This patent substituted a 'chevron or' for a 'chevron argent' and omitted the chained crown from the phoenix of the crest which was made to stand in the rays of the sun. The new motto replaced the old 'As God will so be it'.

The College of Arms recorded the 1610 patent as follows:

Sable a chevron or, between three Crouned Hamers as in the margin herein depicted & for the Creast forth of a Wreath of their Cullors on a hill vert a Phenix proper Fireing her selfe with the sonne beames & by the agitation & working of her winges (according to the Description of Wryters) shee kyndleth certeyne Sticks of Cinamon & other Spices, & therein consumeth her selfe to Ashes, out of which there arriseth another.

This 1610 grant of a patent cost the Blacksmiths £7 12s. *Paide to ye herold att Armes for the renewing of the Armes of this Companye and to his man and for a dynner thereabouts £7 12s.*

In the very early days the Company was to a considerable extent a religious group. Its first hall was lost in 1666 at the time of the Great Fire but the contents were removed in time, and Quest House at Cripplegate was taken over as a hall. The Company was very much a London affair and it was not until the eighteenth century that it admitted 'foreigners', as blacksmiths from outside were called.

The farriers began to organise about the same time as the blacksmiths, but little is known about them from their inception as a Fellowship in the fourteenth century to the granting of a charter by Charles II in 1674 because almost all the Company's records were lost in the Great Fire. The earliest minute book still existing begins in 1719.

But a document of 1356 shows that some form of organisation existed in the mid-fourteenth century:

To Henry Pyracel, Mayor, and the Aldermen of the City of London, shew the good folks, the Master Farriers of the same city, that whereas many offences and great damages had been committed as against persons of the Court and the commonalty of the same city and of all the realm, by people not wise therein, who kept forges in the said city, and intermeddled with the works of farriery, which they did not understand to bring to good end; by reason whereof, many horses had been lost, to the great damage of the people:— therefore the said Mayor caused to be summoned before him all the farriers of the said city, and to be chosen from among them two masters, the most sufficient men, and the best knowing; that is to say Richard de Hertele and John de Oxenford . . . and gave them full power to oversee and govern the same trade.

As a result of this, various rules and penalties were introduced. Any farrier found guilty of poor workmanship had to pay a fine to the chamber of the Guildhall. If after this he transgressed again, he had to 'forswear the same trade within the city for ever'. In addition a member was not allowed to accept gifts when asked advice on buying horses, and might not attempt to perform a cure unless he was reasonably sure of success. Charges had not to be higher than 'they were wont to be before the time of the pestilence' (the Black Death of 1348-50), which was 'a shoe of six nails $1\frac{1}{2}$d and a shoe of eight nails 2d'. The charge for taking off a shoe was fixed at a halfpenny.

The early farriers were also known as 'marshall farriers' or just 'marshalls'. An illuminated pedigree of the Ferrers or Ferrars family which was given to the farriers in 1612 claims that the Company of Farriers is much older than any other records suggest.

For Anncesterie of tyme oh! who canne tell
The first beginning of so old a trade,
For Horsses were before the Deluge fell,
And Cures and shoes, before that tyme were made,
We neede not presse tyme further than it beares,
A Company have Farriers beene 300 yeres!!!

This pedigree of the Ferrers family remained in the possession of the Worshipful Company of Farriers until the nineteenth century, when it was lost. The ancient arms of this family, 'argent, three horses sable', are the same as those of the Company. The pedigree has an illustration of the tools used in farriery at the beginning of the seventeenth century.

The genealogical tree in the pedigree begins with Henry de Ferrers of the eleventh century, who, despite his period, is shown in plate armour of late sixteenth century character. He is lying on his back on a green ground, his visor is raised, he has a plume of feathers on his helmet and covering his right arm is an oval-shaped shield charged with six horseshoes. Immediately above him and on either side of the stem of the tree is this note: *Henrie de Ferrars, or Ferrer, a Norman, whoe came over with William the Conqueror, whoe gave to hyme the honor of Tutbury, in the Countie of Stafforde, wch was the firste howse was given to the Ferrers in England.* Henry de Ferrers is thought to have taken his name from the small town of Ferrieres in France. The area of Ferrieres abounded with iron mines and Henry was possibly in the iron trade.

In 1572 John Xoules left a house in West Smithfield, London, to the churchwardens of St Sepulchre on condition that they paid 13s 4d annual rent to the Farriers Company.

But despite all their claims the farriers did not get a charter until 1674. This, granted by Charles II, stated:

> . . . *Whereas we have beene informed by the humble petition of our wellbeloved subjects the Brotherhood of Farryers within our Cities of London and Westminster that their Art and Trade is of great antiquity and of great use and benefitt to our subjects for preserving of horses and that diverse unexpert and unskilfull persons inhabiting within the liberties of the said citties have of late taken upon them the said Art and Mistery whoe have thereby for want of due knowledge and skill in the right way of preserving of horses destroyed many horses in or neare the same*

Coat of arms of the Worshipful Company of Farriers, showing horseshoes and an arm holding a hammer, 1674

cittyes, and for that the said Brotherhood have not power to search and oversee such as professe the said Art without the liberties of our said cittyes soe that the said abusers doe dayly increase for remedy whereof they have humbly besought us that wee would be graciously pleased to Incorporate them and all others that now lawfully use the said Art and Trade within our said Cities of London and Westminster and the liberties thereof and within seaven miles distant from the same unto a Body Politique and Corporate and to invest them with power and jurisdiction for the well ordering and governing of the said Art and Trade and all such as use or shall use the same within the lymitts aforesaid . . .

The charter ordained that forty-nine named persons should be allowed to join the Company and also all others who at that date 'professed the said Trade, Art or Mistery of a Farryer' and had done so for three years within a seven-mile radius of London and Westminster and had also served an apprenticeship within those limits for seven years.

There was to be a Master, three Wardens and not above

twenty or under ten Assistants. The first Master was Gregory Costen who held the office until 1674, and he was followed by Andrew Snape, Sergeant-Farrier to the King. The first three Wardens were Andrew Snape, Samuell Mabbs and Samuell Dickons. Robert Strugnel was the first clerk.

The armorial bearings were:

Argent three horseshoes sable pierced argent.
Crest: *On a wreath of the colours an arm embowed issuing from clouds on the sinister side all proper, holding in the hand a hammer azure handled and crowned or.*
Mantling: *Sable doubled argent.*
Supporters: *Two horses argent.*
Motto: *Vi et virtute.*

At one time the farriers may have had a hall known as Trinity or Common Hall. But most of the meetings were held in taverns or coffee houses, and these included the *Crown Tavern* and *White Horse* in Cripplegate, *Pope's Head Tavern, George and Vulture Tavern* in Cornhill, *Red Cross* in Red Cross Street, *Guildhall Coffee House, New Castle Coffee House,* in Billings-gate, *Blacksell's Coffee House* of Queen Street, *Badley's Hotel* of Bridge Street, and the *Albion Hotel,* Aldersgate Street.

The farriers are said to have celebrated St Clement's Day at the *White Horse* as late as 1883, when one of the fraternity appeared in a new apron with gilt tags, and a special drink concocted of gin, eggs, ginger and spices was consumed in honour of the Saint.

In later years halls of other Companies were sometimes borrowed or meetings were held at the clerk's office. From 1942 onwards they were held in the Tallow Chandlers Hall in Dowgate Street.

The farriers took part in the Lord Mayor's Procession and the order of the march was the staffmen followed by the 'whifflers' (who cleared the way for processions), the City banner, King's banner, Company standard and Great standard. After that came two 'pendants' (banner-bearers) abreast, musick, beadle and the Master and others in order of seniority.

A report of one Lord Mayor's procession in 1727 says that breakfast was taken before the march and a stop made halfway at 'Mr Burt's' for a glass of wine. When it was all over they sat down to a dinner of 'three leggs of Lamb, three leggs of Veal with Bacon Greens etc., eighteen Fowles some boyled with Oysters and some Roasted, Nine Geese and six Dishes of Tarts.'

The apprentices of the Farriers Company were subject to strict rules:

> *You shall constantly and devoutly, on your Knees, every Day, serve GOD, and make Conscience in the due Hearing of his Word preached, and endeavour the right Practice thereof in your Life and Conversation: Be thinking often upon your Mortality, and be wise to improve your present Time for Eternity: And, when you shall have Leisure from your Master's Business, and shall have your Master's Leave, you shall go to the Public Prayers of the Church, and there behave yourself devoutly. You shall do diligent and faithful Service to your Master, for the Time of your Apprenticeship, and deal truly in what you shall be intrusted with. You shall often read over the Covenants of your Indenture, and see and endeavour to perform the same to the uttermost of your Power. You shall avoid all the Evil Company, and all Occasions which may tend to draw you to the same; and always make speedy Return when you shall be sent of your Master's or Mistress's Errands. You shall avoid Idleness, and be ever employed, either for GOD's Service or in your Master's Business. You shall be of fair, gentle, and lowly Speech and Behaviour to all Men, especially to your Governors, and those that have the rule over you: Then shall you answer your chief End, to wit, the GLORY of GOD, and your own Peace and Happiness, now and for ever.*

The apprentices of the Blacksmiths Company were expected to

An attempt in 1900 to get farriers and blacksmiths to join a trade union

behave just as devoutly as those of the Farriers. They were not supposed to go into taverns or playhouses, to play at dice, cards, or any other unlawful game 'which might cause their masters any loss'. They were not allowed to marry nor were they supposed to 'indulge in fornication'.

As the years went by these London-based Companies failed to meet the everyday needs of the majority of blacksmiths and farriers, and other organisations became necessary. At one time there were five societies in London alone but by 1870 four of these had united into the Permanent Amalgamated Farriers Protection Society, the fifth, the London West-End Farriers Trade Association, going its own way for another four years until it also joined the Permanent Amalgamated. At the meeting when the West-End Farriers decided to join the others it was stated that they were sick of being treated with contempt by the 'gilded chamber in the City, the Worshipful Company of Farriers'.

The Worshipful Company of Farriers did try to improve things but it was never again to be an effective trade organisation. In 1890 it introduced a scheme for the examination and registration of shoeing smiths and later broadened the terms of membership to allow even the village blacksmith to join.

Outside London attempts were also made to organise during the second half of the nineteenth century when it was becoming increasingly hard to make a living. In 1891 the blacksmiths of Manchester set up an Amalgamated Society of Farriers and Blacksmiths, which soon had branches in Blackburn, Burnley and other Lancashire towns. Yorkshire also set up a similar organisation with branches in Leeds, Huddersfield and Halifax. In 1894 the two counties amalgamated and joined forces with the midland branches who had organised themselves under the banner of the Birmingham and District Shoeing Smiths' Protection Society. Another organisation, the Yorkshire County Shoeing Smith Association, was also energetic in defence of its members.

These protection societies set out to keep the standard of work high and this meant that they had to stop the cutting of prices which was going on in many areas. Members were also not supposed to touch any work that had been done by non-members. A typical rule was:

You must not fasten a horse's loose shoes, nor replace any that have been knocked out by contact with tramlines or

*other street obstacles, unless such shoes have been origin-
ally supplied by a member.*

In 1902 the National Master Farriers' Association was formed
and in 1919 changed its name to the National Master Farriers'
and Blacksmiths' Association. Later 'Agricultural Engineers' was
added to the title.

In Scotland the Scottish Corporation of Hammermen holds
records as far back as 1582 and has existed since 1483 at least.
Blacksmiths could belong to the Hammermen but to do so they
had to make 'ane door cruick and door band, ane iron spade,
ane schoile [shovel], one horse shoe and six nails thereto'.

The Hammermen were a looser organisation than most of the
others and even amateur tradesmen seem to have been able to
join, for in 1657 Charles Smith, Advocate, a son of the Lord
Provost of Edinburgh, was admitted as a blacksmith on his sub-
mitting 'the portrait of a horse's leg, shoed with a silver shoe,
fixed with three nails, with silver staple at the end thereof.' But
all had to swear a solemn oath which began, 'I shall serve my
customers in my vocation without fraud or guile', and ended,
'I shall not seduce any of my brethren's apprentices or servants
nor employ them before they have a proper clearance from their
masters.' And no Hammerman, either master or servant, was
allowed to practise more than one craft.

After World War II when riding clubs, hunts, races and pony
clubs brought back interest in the horse an effort was made to
get young men to train to become blacksmiths and farriers. By
1959 the Herefordshire College of Further Education had organised a course of training in the craft. In 1962 the Worshipful
Company of Farriers launched an apprenticeship scheme which
gave bursaries and grants to augment the basic wages paid
during the four or five years of apprenticeship. This scheme
was for young men wanting to specialise in farriery and the Company was helped financially in its efforts by the Horserace
Betting Levy Board, while other support came from sources
such as the Riding Clubs Committee of the British Horse Society,

the British Show Jumping Association and the Pony Club, together with the continued backing of the British Horse Society Coaching Club, Hackney Horse Society, Horse and Pony Benefit Society, Jockey Club, London Harness Horse Parade Society, National Master Farriers', Blacksmiths' and Agricultural Engineers' Association, Ponies of Britain Club and the Thoroughbred Breeders Association. The Royal Army Veterinary Corps also helped.

To supplement the donations and to pay the running costs of the scheme the Worshipful Company of Farriers also launched an appeal for funds from its own liverymen.

Other blacksmiths turned from shoeing horses and, helped by the Rural Industries Bureau (later the Council for Small Industries in Rural Areas), concentrated on decorative ironwork.

A national apprenticeship scheme was also started by the National Joint Apprenticeship Council for the Farriery, Blacksmiths' and Agricultural Engineering Trade and this catered particularly for the country blacksmith. In Scotland, the Scottish Country Industries Development Trust helped many a village blacksmith.

The Herefordshire College of Further Education provides full facilities for training to become blacksmiths and farriers. The young apprentice fashioning the horseshoe has just completed the course

3

The Craft of the Blacksmith

'A working smith all other trades excels'
Anonymous: *Ode on Smithery*, 1610

Forging is one of the oldest and best ways of making objects from iron and steel, for metal forged at the correct temperature retains all its strength. When metal is forged it is heated until soft and then hammered into shape before it cools and sets again.

Wrought iron has long been regarded as the traditional material for the blacksmith but nowadays he generally uses mild steel (which is a tough strong alloy of pure iron and carbon).

Wrought iron is produced by puddling pig iron in a special hearth and is more expensive than mild steel. Commercial wrought iron contains about 0·04 per cent of carbon and 0·2 per cent of slag. During the manufacturing process the carbon and slag are hammered or squeezed throughout the mass of the metal to form a fibrous structure which is given the name wrought iron. Wrought iron can easily be recognised by being broken across the grain to expose this fibrous structure.

There are two vital qualities in wrought iron—ductility,

The Blacksmith, by W. Biscombe Gardner, 1883

which means that it can be drawn out when hot, and malleability, which allows it to be hammered to any desired shape. Not all wrought iron is of top quality: an excess of phosphorus and sulphur in the metal can produce what is termed 'cold short', a type of iron liable to break when cold; while an excess of silicon, on the other hand, can produce 'red short' iron, which is liable to break when hot. Wrought iron is preferred for decorative ironwork for several reasons: it can be worked at a wider range of temperatures than mild steel, its texture improves with forging and it can be worked and welded into intricate, delicate and graceful shapes. The term 'wrought ironwork' has become the definition of a method rather than a material and can be used to describe any article in iron or mild steel which shows that the fire and hammer have been used. But the shaping of metal by sawing or oxyacetylene cutting is excluded from wrought ironwork, as are the bending of bars when cold and any welding carried out by electric arc or oxyacetylene methods.

Steel is a general term applied to alloys of pure iron and carbon and its quality is determined by selecting the iron and the alloying ingredients used in its manufacture. It is not determined by the content of carbon or by its appearance when fractured: the temper of steel refers to the carbon content and has nothing to do with the quality of the steel.

Mild steel contains from 0·2 to 0·3 per cent of carbon. It is less ductile and malleable than wrought iron but has the advantage of possessing greater tensile strength. It can also be readily forged and welded within a narrower range of temperature, but it cannot be hardened or tempered. When fractured, it shows a granular structure as opposed to the fibrous structure of wrought iron.

Other steels can be used. Medium-carbon steel containing 0·5 to 0·6 per cent is harder and stronger than mild steel but, although easy to forge, is not readily welded. High-carbon steel possesses 0·75 to 1·5 per cent of carbon and can be tempered to retain a cutting edge. There is also a wide range of alloy steels.

For the making of horseshoes the iron usually comes in 18 foot concave bars graded according to their section. For very heavy shoes the bar is plain without fullering for the nails, the nails being individually countersunk below the surface. Plain iron in preferred for heavy work especially for farm horses working on the land, for plain shoes do not collect so much soil.

A forge can mean the blacksmith shop or the smithy itself but more correctly the name should be applied to the hearth or fire. It is rectangular, usually made of brick but sometimes of iron,

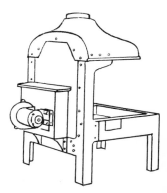

Rear view of a smith's hearth of cast iron, showing the cowl to take away the smoke and fumes

and on it the blacksmith builds his pit or bed of coal or coke breeze. Over the pit is a cowl or canopy of brick or sheet iron, designed to take away the smoke and fumes; though at times the smoke produced in a blacksmith's shop is far too much to be absorbed in this way.

At the end of the hearth farthest from the fire there is a trough of water for cooling tools, hardening and tempering iron-work and containing the fire. It is sometimes known as the bosh.

Whether coal or coke breeze is used for the fire depends generally on local custom or on the availability of the respective fuels. Good smithy coal should be bituminous and free from sulphur.

Tools for the hearth include a poker, shovel, rake and swab though some blacksmiths dispense with the rake and swab. The shovel is sometimes given the name of slice; it is a long-handled, light, nearly flat shovel for scooping up the fuel and arranging it around and over the fire. For cooling and containing the fire with water a perforated can fastened to a long iron handle may be used, or a bunch of twigs.

The air to keep the fire burning comes from a hand-driven bellows or a mechanical blower usually in a recess behind the hearth. In old village forges there were often two bellows so that the blacksmith and his assistant could each work on one side of the hearth, where they had their own anvil and set of tools. Most bellows have a double action so that a blast of air is produced both on the downward and upward strokes. The cow's

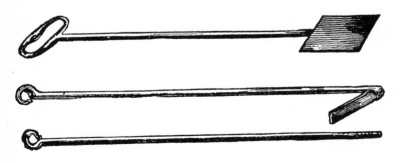

Tools for the hearth: (*above*) shovel or slice; (*below*) rake and poker

horn seen on the end of many a bellows' lever (and shown in the illustration on page 55) is to give a good grip and is particularly liked because it keeps clean and is very hard wearing. Bellows are thought to have originated from a goatskin with a small opening, into which was fitted a hollow reed or clay pipe. The early bellows operators used two goatskins and pressed each in turn with their foot. In either hand they held a leather thong attached to the upper surface of the goatskin and by alternately transferring their weight from one skin to the other they operated a rhythmic and effective bellows. Bellows menders toured the country repairing damage.

The experienced blacksmith can obtain a wide range of heats by skilful use of the bellows and the coal or breeze. The names given to these heats are 'warm' when the heated iron is just not hot enough to glow in shadow, and 'black' when it glows very faintly; and these are followed in order by such self-explanatory named heats as cherry-red, dull-red, blood-red, bright-red, and bright-yellow. Other heats (for welding) have names like snowball, full, light, slippery, greasy and sweating.

In the blacksmith's fire, clinker is the worst enemy, for when hot it is like black treacle and when cold it turns to something like crude black glass. It has to be kept out of the fire and this is done by letting it cool sufficiently and hooking it out with a curved-point poker.

After a hearth, the most important large item in a black-smith's shop is the anvil. The first anvils were probably lumps of crude iron ore but over the centuries a definite pattern has evolved.

Today anvils are made of wrought iron or mild steel with a specially hardened surface. The two main patterns are the London and the Peter Wright. A good anvil weighs up to three hundredweight. It needs to be good, for working on a poor one can be compared with jumping in a heap of sand, while working on a good one is like jumping on to a spring-board, the rebound from each blow of the hammer helping

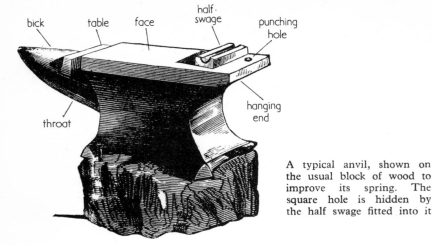

A typical anvil, shown on the usual block of wood to improve its spring. The square hole is hidden by the half swage fitted into it

toward the next.

The London anvil, which is the more common, has a face, table, bick, throat and hanging end. The face is the large flat surface, and the bick is the cone-shaped projection used for curving pieces of iron, shaping horseshoes, making rings and so on. The curved underpart of the bick is the throat. Next to the bick is a fairly small flat area, the table, the surface of which has not been specially hardened like the rest of the anvil surface, and which is used when iron is being cut with a cold chisel to prevent the edge of the chisel from being damaged by passing through the iron on to the surface below.

At the end of the face opposite to the table and bick and on the hanging end there are two holes, one round, the other square. The round one is a punching hole, sometimes known as a pritchel hole. It is usually less than one inch in diameter and is designed to take the shanks of various tools and to receive the point of any tool being used to punch holes into hot iron, as when making nail holes in horseshoes.

The square hole is a hardie or swage hole. A hardie is a chisel, and a swage is a top and bottom tool between which iron is worked to shape. The hardie and the bottom half of the swage fit into the square hole, which also takes the square shanks of various other tools that make their impact on the undersides of the work when struck from above.

The anvil is best placed on a block of wood for this improves its spring. A squared-up trunk of elm is preferable, and the block should be set some three feet at least into the ground, with the grain standing vertical and the height of the anvil arranged to suit the blacksmith. It must also be set at the correct distance and angle from the hearth or the blacksmith will do a great deal of unnecessary work. The face is generally arranged so that it slopes away slightly from the user, for this allows the metal scales to fall away from the object being hammered.

A bench equipped with vices and a drill is a main part of the smithy and on this are kept most of the tools. One of the vices is usually a steel leg vice; this allows the strain and shock at the jaws to be taken by the leg, which is often let into a steel socket on the floor. For lighter work a paralleled-jaw or engineer's vice is often used.

A floor-mandrel is a hollow-cast cone, often standing breast high, which is used for true-ing up small hoops, rings, iron tyres and so on.

A swage-block is a heavy block of cast iron with differing kinds or sizes of slots, holes and grooves in the sides and through the face. It is used as a kind of auxiliary anvil to shape pieces of metal.

The principal tools are hand and sledge hammers, chisels,

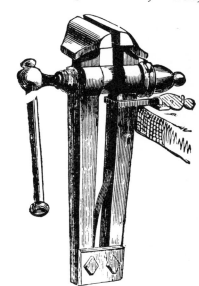

Steel leg vice

drills, punches, and a selection of tongs with variously shaped jaws.

The two main hammers are the straight or cross-peen and the ball-peen. The former, which weighs about two pounds, has a haft of about twelve inches and its steel head has one side slightly convex and the other wedge-shaped. The angle of the wedge decides whether the hammer is called straight or cross. The ball-peen is the blacksmith's general purpose hammer; it is much like the cross-peen but with a snub nose at the rear of the striking face end. It is from one and threequarter pounds to three pounds in weight and the balance is carefully tested to suit the individual blacksmith.

The sledge is the heavy hammer used by the striker, who is generally the blacksmith's chief assistant. Its weight can be seven, twelve or twenty pounds and it has a haft of hickory a good yard long. It must be well made to stand up to the heavy work it has to do.

With the ball-peen and the sledge the blacksmith and his assistant work in rhythm, the smaller hammer indicating where and when the sledge must make its massive strokes. The signal for the sledge to stop is a lighter tap of the smaller hammer on the face of the anvil away from the object being hammered.

There are various shafted tools which the smith uses to bring the metal to the shape he requires. Some have chisel-like edges for cutting hot or cold metal, some are used for smoothing or flattening its surface and others have square or round edges for forging inside corners. There are also forming tools, which make rounded grooves in the metal, and swages made in two parts for forging rounded portions.

Punches and drifts of various types and sizes are used for making holes, a punch being used to start the hole and a drift to make it larger and to shape it and give it clear edges.

For measuring and checking his work the smith uses dividers, callipers and a rule made of brass so that it will not rust nor discolour with heat and become unreadable. If he is making a

Blacksmith and striker, the latter holding the heavy hammer or sledge. The huge bellows were controlled by the hanging lever. From *The Boy's Book of Trades*, 1888

number of articles of the same size he may use a template or pattern to guide him in his forging, or a special gauge with which to check his work quickly.

In the actual forging the blacksmith may use only a hammer or he may employ a combination of tools: it will depend on what he is making and the shape of the metal he is making it from.

All the time he watches the changing colour of the metal: when it is in the fire he must be able to judge not only when it has reached the correct heat for working but also whether or not it is reaching it at the right speed. The changes of colour give him the information he needs. If the metal is kept in the fire too long it begins to burn and form scaly lumps. The spoiled metal then has to be cut off and thrown away, which means a loss of both time and material.

When the metal has reached the correct heat for forging, the smith withdraws it from the fire and, unless it is a long piece which he can handle safely at the cold end, he uses tongs to hold it. Before starting to forge he removes any scale which has formed by knocking it off with his hammer or using a wire brush.

Ornamental ironwork today is mostly in the hands of specialists but the ordinary village blacksmith should be able to make a decorative sign or, say, an iron gate of simple design. The specialist—the artist in iron—generally works to full scale drawings, tracing each design through paper treated with chalk on to a large metal plate on which he later checks his scrolls against the chalk lines. The scrolls are made by fixing the hot bar in a vice and bending it with a scroll wrench—and it requires a skilled craftsman to judge the correct length of bar to make a scroll. To help him estimate the length needed the smith may use a piece of soft wire, which he first bends round all the curves of the drawing, then straightens and measures. Shoulders or printed corners are forged on the anvil using the flat of the anvil top and its edges, the curves of the bick and a set hammer to

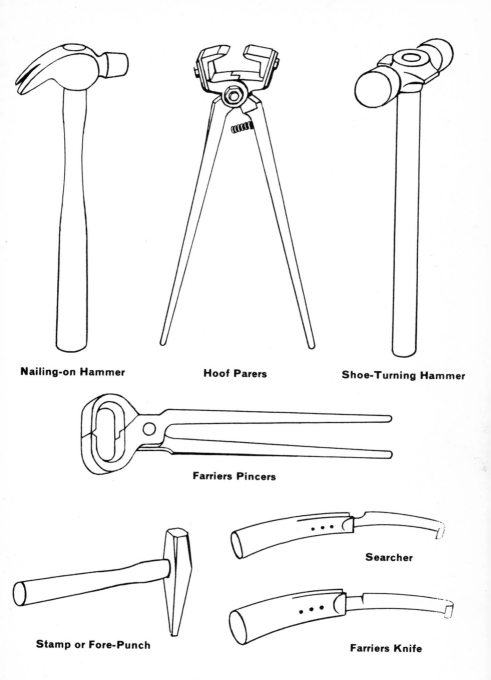

Nailing-on Hammer   **Hoof Parers**   **Shoe-Turning Hammer**

Farriers Pincers

Searcher

Stamp or Fore-Punch

Farriers Knife

Farrier's tools

give the bar the desired shape.

The making of imitation leaves is difficult work. If only a few leaves similar to each other are to be made the smith will forge each by hand on the anvil, spreading the bar or strip to the necessary size, hammering it to shape on the curved surface of the bick or with forming tools on the anvil top and then 'chasing' the finished leaf to make the veins. Where, however, a lot of identical leaves are to be made a set of dies may be provided. The twisting of the bars is usually done cold by fixing each bar in a vice and twisting it with a special wrench.

Having made the different parts of the design the ironwork craftsman has to join them together. This he formerly did by fire welding or by riveting, but nowadays oxyacetylene or electric arc-welding is more generally practised.

But as the village blacksmith is, or at least was, almost always a farrier—one who shoes horses—as well, he needs additional tools for this purpose. A farrier's nailing-on hammer is one with a light slightly curved and whippy haft and a small boss-like face opposite a curved double claw. The claw is use to twist off the point of a nail where it projects after having been driven into the horse's hoof. Many of the tongs are made by the blacksmith and have descriptive names such as wide, flat, square, round, half-round, open mouth, closed mouth, hollow bit and shoeing. The handles are a fairly uniform twenty inches in length. He also needs pincers for extracting nails, a hoof-clipper or hoof-parer for clipping off unwanted material from the hoof, and buffers and rasps and a paring knife for preparing the hoof.

The paring knife, which has a short curved blade set in a stumpy handle, has a tip with an angled hook; a smaller version is often known as a searcher.

The farrier has his box equipped with the tools and nails necessary for taking off and fitting of shoes. The nails are No 12 (3 inches long, for heavy draught horses), No 6 (2 inches long, for hunters) and No 3 ($1\frac{3}{4}$ inches long, for racehorses). Shoes vary in weight: a heavy draught horse needs shoes weigh-

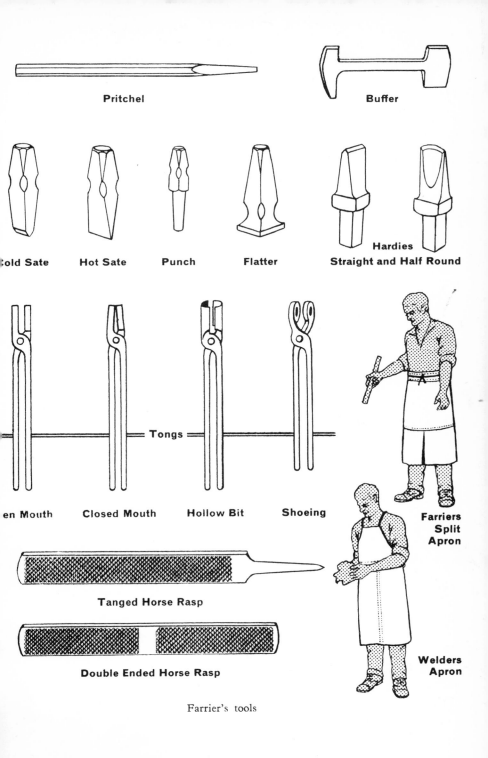

Pritchel

Buffer

Cold Sate

Hot Sate

Punch

Flatter

Hardies
Straight and Half Round

Tongs

Open Mouth

Closed Mouth

Hollow Bit

Shoeing

Farriers Split Apron

Tanged Horse Rasp

Double Ended Horse Rasp

Welders Apron

Farrier's tools

ing around 4lb each and secured by four nails on either side, while racing and hunting horses need shoes weighing from 9 to 14 ounces and secured by four nails on the outside and three on the inside. Shoes for a donkey or mule have the points a little extended and turned slightly out.

When a horse is brought in for shoeing it is generally tied to a ring-bolt on the wall of the smithy. Awkward horses are often given a nose-bag to keep them occupied and a young horse being shod for the first time is often accompanied by an older one. The farrier examines the fore feet first so that the horse will not be nervous. He taps the foot to tell the horse which one is needed and then he lays his hand on the fore foot and gently slides the hand down to the hoof. This seems automatically to make the horse raise its foot. A special three-footed iron stand shown in the frontispiece and on page 127, with a smooth polished top is available for the horse to rest its fore foot when being shod.

Shoeing the hind feet is more difficult and more tiring for the farrier. Because he is out of the horse's vision the horse can tend to become restive and as it can send the iron stand flying this is rarely used to rest the hind feet. The foot is taken in the lap of the leather apron as the blacksmith bends beneath the haunches of the horse with his back to the animal.

Clinched ends of shoe-nails are knocked off and the nails pulled out with pincers. The hoof is rasped and picked clean and pared with the knife. The shoe is heated and tried for size and this make a dense smoke which gives a smithy its characteristic smell. The cold shoe is then nailed on, starting from the front, and the nails are clinched where they protrude. Finally the hoofs are given a dressing of oil and paraffin to make them look good and the horse is ready to go home.

A good blacksmith rarely uses force and seldom raises his voice, though an especially recalcitrant animal can try the patience of the best of them. A soothing voice achieves more than all the shouting.

4

Strange and Strong Smiths

He's knight o' war, and lord o' love,
And king o' a' the shire, man'
Anonymous: *The Smith's a Gallant Fireman*

'Lord of the Elves' he was called by some; he was the son of
a mermaid and the sea-giant Wate, and his uncle was King
Vilkinus. He was well known in Scandinavian, German and
Anglo-Saxon tradition. His name was Wayland Smith.

He was a smith of outstanding skill. He had been bound
apprentice to the smith Mimir, who employed dwarfs to work
for him, and the story goes that Wayland very quickly sur-
passed the dwarfs at their work. He lived for seven years in
Ulfdaler with his brothers Eigil the Archer and Slagfidr and
three swan-maidens. Then he was captured by the Swedish king
Nidude (Nithad, Niduth, Nidune), who hamstrung him to prevent his running away and put him to work in the royal smithy.

Wayland bided his time for revenge, but when he did take it
it was a terrible one. He killed the king's two sons, made drinking bowls out of their skulls, and sent them to their father the
king. When the king's daughter Bödvild brought a gold ring to

the smithy to be mended he raped her.

Before he could be caught he flew away on wings which he had made himself out of birds' feathers. These wings had earlier been tried out by Wayland's brother Eigil, but Eigil had been killed in the attempt.

The Franks casket, a carved whalebone box of eighth-century Northumbrian workmanship (now in the British Museum) is thought to illustrate Wayland's legend. It shows him at work with the head of one of the king's sons grasped in his lap while the headless body lies on the ground below the anvil. With his right hand he is extending a cup, perhaps made from the skull of the other son, to the daughter Bödvild whom he raped. Bödvild, on the casket, is accompanied by a servant holding the gold ring which has been brought to be mended.

For centuries Wayland has been one of Britain's popular mythical figures. A long barrow near White Horse Hill, Berkshire, is reputed to be his stone burial chamber. The great victory of King Alfred over the Danish invaders took place near this spot in Berkshire and the burial place of Baereg, the Danish chieftain who was slain in this battle, is marked by a heap of stones less than a mile from White Horse Hill. On the east side

of the hill is the group of stones which form a small cave known as Wayland's Smithy, or Wayland's Cave. It is mentioned as early as AD 850.

A local legend says that the place is haunted by an invisible smith who will shoe a horse for a traveller provided that a coin is left on a stone and that the traveller goes away while the work is in progress. If he tries to watch, or looks towards the smithy, nothing happens.

Wayland's story is told in the 'Volundarkviōa', one of the poems in the *Poetic Edda,* and, with variations, in the *Diōreks Saga.* He is also mentioned in the Anglo-Saxon poems *Waldere* and *The Lament of Deor,* in *Beowulf,* and in a note inserted by Alfred the Great into his translation of *Boethius.*

The name ·probably comes from the Old English Weland, the Old Norse Volundr and the German Wieland. The Anglo-Saxon 'welan' meant 'to fabricate'.

Before going into battle, Beowulf asks that there should be sent to Higelac:

My garments of battle,
The best that my bosom bears,
The richest of my clothes,
The remains of the Hred-lan,
The work of Weland.

In a French poem thought to be of the seventh century it is said that the armour made by 'Veland' had not been able to save the hero Randolph from death. Gautier de Vascastein, in the legend *De Prima Expeditione Attlae Regis Hunorum Gallias,* carried arms made by 'Veland'.

A chronicle of the twelfth century relates how Count William of Angoulême was nicknamed Taillefer after his sword, which had been made by 'Welander', and with which he cut in two a warrior encased in full armour. Count William is said to have struck the first blow at the Battle of Hastings and died on horseback as he dashed into the enemy's ranks.

Opposite: Wayland Smith's cave in Berkshire

Der Schmidt, a German woodcut by Jost Amman, 1535-91

There were other blacksmiths like Wayland Smith. The brothers Grimm tell the story of how in the Detterberg mountains not far from Munster dwelt a wild man Grinken the Smith. He lived underground in a deep cave where he had his forge. His workmanship was said to be so perfect that it lasted for ever and no lock made by him could be opened without the proper key.

John Gay in his *Trivia* writes of another:

Far in the lane a lonely hut he found,
No tenant ventured on the unwholesome ground;
Here smokes his forge, he bares his sinewy arm,
And early strokes the sounding anvil warm;
Around his shop the steely sparkles flew,
As for the steed he shaped the bending shoe.

In the eleventh century a man named Cobbe was a black-smith at Eling in the New Forest. The Manor of Eling belonged to the kings of England and the blacksmith held his land on condition that when the king visited the forest he was to supply the royal visitor with arrows and horseshoes. King William Rufus, staying at Eling, decided to do a day's hunting in the forest and Cobbe dutifully presented his fee of shoes and six arrows. Rufus kept four arrows and gave the other two to Sir Walter Tyrrell. The royal party moved off to Stoney Cross where Rufus was killed by an arrow. Cobbe identified the arrow as one of the two that had been given to Tyrrell, thus proving that it was this knight who had killed the king. At Tyrrell's Ford near Sopley there is an old blacksmith's shop reputed to be the place where Sir Walter Tyrrell's horse was shod with shoes pointing backwards to mislead his pursuers.

In 1497 a blacksmith, Michael Joseph, from St Keverne in Cornwall led an army to Blackheath to lay siege to London in protest against Henry VII's taxes. The rebels were defeated and Joseph was executed. Today he is one of the heroes of Cornish nationalists.

One of the oldest smithies to exist in modern times was at Barrasford in Northumberland where from the days of Bannock-burn, over 600 years ago, the Urwins practised their trade until World War II. Near Barrasford runs the geat Roman highway to the north and a short distance away stand the remains of the great wall of Hadrian. No doubt, even in Roman times, black-smiths would have been working in that area. Other members of the Urwin family practised their trade in nearby Northumbrian villages.

In *Tales of a Grandfather* Sir Walter Scott tells the story of one of the Macdonalds who robbed a poor widow in the far north of Scotland and nailed horseshoes to her feet. When her wounds were healed she went to Edinburgh and asked the help of King James I in righting her wrongs. The king caused Macdonald and twelve of his men to be seized, had them shod in the same manner as they had shod the woman, and caused them to be publicly exhibited for three days before being executed.

A similar story comes from Russia. In 1897 a village blacksmith by the name of Nicolas Temliakoff, being jealous of his wife, made her a pair of well-fitting iron horseshoes which he proceeded to nail to her feet 'heedless of her fearful screams and prayers for mercy'. Temliakoff's idea may have been that if his wife was fond of running after other men she should not wear out shoe leather at his expense. When she swooned under the extreme torture he revived her by pricking her neck and shoulders with a sharp knife. The incident is alleged to have taken place at Bolshe-Kosulski near Tomsk, but one suspects some exaggeration in the story because, after being locked up for a couple of days by his fellow villagers, this farrier of human beings was set at liberty.

Mackie's Smithy in Aitken Street, Largs, Scotland, was founded in 1608 by Robert Mackie. The original building stood until this century and the anvil was one on which shoes had been made for the horses of people who flocked into the town for the centuries-old Colms Fair. The inscription on the façade of the smithy read: 'R.A.M.—1608—M.F.', the initials being those of Robert A. Mackie and of Margaret Findlay his wife. Stage coach and postgig horses employed in the delivery of mail between Ayr and Greenock were serviced by this firm. One Sunday when the mail coach was about to pass through, a horse cast a shoe just before getting into Largs. Mackie the blacksmith was in church listening to the sermon

Blacksmith, by Randolph Caldecott. From *The Graphic* of 1876

when someone came and whispered that he was wanted. He left immediately and shod the horse—Sabbath or not the mail had to get through.

Arms were forged on the old anvil for the Chartist Rising which never came, with the result that later the swords had to be beaten back into ploughshares. Probably the claymores of earlier days also received the necessary attention on this anvil.

In 1930 Mackie's moved to Boyd Street where they took

'Ye Loyal Blacksmith of Marlborough.' An engraving of the author from
*A Genuine and Faithfull Account of the Sufferings of William Haulbrook
Blacksmith in the reign of King Charles First . . . written by himself
during his confinement*, 1744

over another old blacksmith business, that of Frazer. Frazer, at one time, had his own boat for taking ploughs and other implements to the islands of Bute and Cambrae. Farming implements made at Frazer's were sent as far as New Zealand and were packed in seed corn, ostensibly to protect the machinery but mainly because the corn could be exported in that way without being liable to duty. Over the smithy door were the figures of Burn's Tam O'Shanter and Soutar Johnny, no doubt because a blacksmith had been Tam's and Soutar Johnny's drinking mate.

Two engravings dated 1744 and 1749 are all that now remain of a portrait of a certain William Haulbrook or Hoolbrook which is said to have been painted in 1659. William Haulbrook was a blacksmith at Marlborough in Wiltshire in the reign of Charles I.

During the period between the end of Richard Cromwell's protectorship and the return of the king a desperate attempt was made by a group of republican officers to take over the country again and to keep down the rising hopes of the king's party. William Haulbrook became mixed up in this affair. He later told his story and proclaimed his innocence in *A Genuine and Faithfull Account of the Sufferings of William Haulbrook Blacksmith in the reign of King Charles First . . . written by himself during his confinement*. London 1744.

This work has the running title 'A Blacksmith and no Jesuit or the Smith of Marlborough'. The engraving forms the frontispiece and has the legend at the top: 'By hamer and hand all arts do stand', which is the motto of the Blacksmiths Company.

Below the portrait is written:

Se Will *ye loyal* Black-Smith *who Pris'ner was in Chains,*
But that Bloody Rogue Bradshaw *was hang'd for his pains.*

That 'Bloody Rogue Bradshaw' was the man who examined Haulbrook in London and had him confined to Newgate Prison in chains.

From the blacksmith's story it can be gathered that at Marlborough in the weeks before the Restoration the authorities

were on the alert for any sign of favour of the exiled king. Haulbrook, being a blacksmith, was naturally expected to know the
feelings of the townsfolk—who were for, and who were against,
Richard Cromwell. In July 1659 several of Cromwell's soldiers
came to the town and Haulbrook had the task of shoeing their
horses. After he had shod the horse of Cornet Joyce, this officer
took him into *The White Hart* and gave him plenty to drink in
the hope of getting information. Next day he was sent for again
—this time to *The George*. When he told his mother where he
was going she said, 'Ah! William . . . to *The George* for shoeing,
to *The George* for undoing, I fear.'

And so it turned out. Cornet Joyce had decided that Haulbrook would be useful in London as an informant and had made
plans to capture him. The shoeing done, the drinking began
again, and when Haulbrook had had more than enough one of
the Cromwellian soldiers persuaded him to ride with him to the
end of the town 'to witness the receipt of some money'. Other
soldiers rode along with them and as soon as they were outside
the town they tied Haulbrook's legs under his horse and galloped
off with him to Newbury, where he was transferred to a public
conveyance and taken to London.

After a period in Newgate Prison he was released and when,
soon after, King Charles returned to power William Haulbrook,
according to report, 'lived in Marlborough town . . . a man of
some renown'.

There were blacksmiths of renown in Wales also. William
Cornock of Manorwen who died in 1936 was of a long line of
blacksmiths who had been in Pembrokeshire since before 1680,
in which year Robert Cornock, blacksmith, was imprisoned for his
religious beliefs. William's grandfather was a poet.

Some of the early blacksmiths are best known through iron-
work which they left behind them as a memorial. Tijou the
Frenchman, who made the screens at Hampton Court and St
Paul's Cathedral, had a great influence on wrought-iron workers.
Robert Bakewell, who produced splendid wrought ironwork in the

eighteenth century, remains much of a mystery, for very little is known of his parentage, his life or his death. He may have been apprenticed to Tijou. But he is known to have been at work about 1711 on the curious 'arbour' which still stands in the garden at Melbourne Hall in Derbyshire. At that period he was also doing work for Lord Chesterfield at Bretby and for Earl Ferrers at Staunton Harrold. Yet according to a letter in the Melbourne papers (published by the Historical Manuscripts Commission) he was so poor at that period that he could not take over a shop he had acquired in the town of Derby. Among his work are the chancel screens and gates at Derby Cathedral, the font cover in St Werburgh's Church, and gates at Tissington, Cannock and Worcester.

Thomas, a thirteenth-century blacksmith of Leighton in Bedfordshire, was famous for his ironwork and it was he who was employed to make the 'Eleanor Grille' at Westminster Abbey. The Exchequer Queen Remembrancer accounts (1293-4) record the payment of £13 'to Master Thomas de Leghton, Smith, for ironwork about the tomb of the Queen at Westminster and the expenses of the said Thomas and his men dwelling in London to place the said ironwork about the tomb aforesaid'.

We have the record of another blacksmith who in later years also decorated a tomb in Westminster Abbey. He was D. J. Williams, of Porth-yr-Aur, Caernarvon, who supplied eight handles, a breast plate and an attachment of a sword all made from an antique design. And in the twentieth century blacksmith A. Carne of Truro in Cornwall carried on the tradition with exhibitions of his work in Britain, France and America and specimens of his work in Truro Cathedral; as did the Rathbones of Tongham in Oxfordshire whose wrought ironwork included the Royal Enclosure Gates at Ascot Racecourse. Other names to become famous were Barry, Mitchell and Black of Pyecombe in Sussex and John Jones of Manchester. In 1970 Eric Stevenson, a blacksmith of Wroxham in Norfolk, was admitted to the freedom of the Livery of the Worshipful Company of Blacksmiths and given a gold medal for his 'superb craftsmanship' in making the wrought-iron screens erected in the ancient church of St Nicholas at Great Yarmouth.

Blacksmiths, because of the nature of the job, attracted and produced many strong men. Robert Prometheus Fitzsimmons, who became middleweight boxing champion of the world, was born at Helston in Cornwall. 'Bob' went to New Zealand in 1881, stayed there nine years and then went to America. He was a practising blacksmith most of his life and even when in serious training would make a few horseshoes every day. He had 360 fights in all but his most famous and sensational was in 1897 when he met 'Gentleman Jim' Corbett for the world title. Corbett at the time was heavyweight champion of the world.

On St Patrick's Day, 1897, 20,000 people went to the small gold-rush town of Carson City to watch the fight. Special armed constables were on duty as senators, hoboes, Indians, gold miners, Chinese, Negroes and many others filled the area. As a precaution all weapons were confiscated. It was a fight to the finish for the world title and £4,000 at stake, winner take all. Moving pictures of the fight were taken with a kinetoscope—the first time a fight had been so recorded.

The two competitors hated each other and even had to be prevented from fighting in the hotel lobby before the real encounter began. The newspapers took sides and many harsh things were said and written. In many ways Bob Fitzsimmons was a freak. He had tremendous shoulders and a massive chest but he had knock-knees, thin legs and a peculiar build which made him ungainly and awkward.

The two men climbed into the ring where Fitzsimmons ignored an offer from Corbett to shake hands. The fight began. Corbett, an orthodox fighter, was cool and confident. Fitzsimmons was too slow and his spidery legs coud not match the side-stepping, bobbing, weaving 'Gentleman Jim' whose mocking smile gradually roused Fitzsimmons to such a fury that he seemed incapable of boxing scientifically. At the end of the fifth round only sheer courage was keeping Fitzsimmons on his feet. His arms were flailing the air and he was being battered almost to insensibility.

In the sixth round Fitzsimmons went down to a powerful left to the chin. He rose at the count of nine but to his supporters it seemed all over. In the following round he was driven round the ring and blood began to spurt from a split mouth. Then, through his agony, Bob Fitzsimmons heard a woman's voice screaming, 'Hit him in the slats, Bob. You'll never hit his head!' He recognised his wife's voice and half stepping back, he made a tremendous effort and drove a left into Corbett's side with all the strength he could muster. The blow hurt Corbett considerably and the mocking smile left his face. He staggered and while he was recovering Fitzsimmons's strength began to return.

By the fourteenth round Corbett in his turn was being punched

Nineteenth-century blacksmith using a sledge hammer. By W. Small, 1883

round the ring and eventually took a tremendous blow to the solar plexus which made him shake all over and throw up his hands. Fitzsimmons smashed a right to the jaw and Corbett went to the floor. He tried to heave himself upright to beat the count but collapsed—a beaten man.

Weight-lifting comes naturally to blacksmiths and many have taken this up as a sport. The most famous was Joe Price of Gloucester who not only became a champion blacksmith but also achieved the fame of heavyweight champion weight-lifter of Great Britain.

Born at Stonehouse, Gloucester, Joseph Charles Price was the youngest of eleven children. From his earliest days it seemed obvious that Joe was destined to be phenomenally strong. At birth he weighed fourteen pounds and by the time he was fifteen he was fourteen stone. In his prime he weighed over eighteen stone but even as an old man he had little spare flesh on his body. He was 5ft 10½ inches tall with a chest measurement of fifty-three inches and an expansion of ten inches. He took size twenty in collars. When he left school at fourteen Joe became apprentice to J. Sirrett, a blacksmith of Stonehouse. During World War I he served with the Gloucestershire Yeomanry and in the Royal Army Veterinary Corps as a staff-sergeant farrier-instructor. After the war he was for a time at Minchinhampton, then set up in business at Bearland in Gloucester. The Bearland forge was at the bottom of Longsmith Street, which recalls the past history of Gloucester town when this was the street of the Roman smiths.

Joe Price acquired a great reputation as a shoeing-smith. His natural strength was allied to a professional skill by which in 1920 at the Royal Agricultural Show, he ultimately obtained the highest honour his trade could award—Champion Blacksmith of All England.

As either competitor or judge, Joe attended horse shows all over England. During the course of a hard-working life he found time to assemble a remarkable collection of horseshoes, among them some of Roman and medieval date dug up near his forge. A selection of 300 of these is now in the Gloucester Folk Museum. He took a great interest in horses and prided himself on being able to make any kind of shoe—particularly for a horse with a diseased or injured foot. He early realised the difficulties horses were up against in obtaining a grip on the new tarmacadam roads and, besides writing about the theoretical aspects of the problem, he experimented with various types of material beneath the shoe to give the horse a better foothold.

He certainly had a way with horses. In his early days he would shoe the horses, slap them on the flanks and tell them to go home on their own. And off they would go, trotting along, and the policemen would see their new shoes and let them proceed.

The famous blacksmith tackled many jobs in his day, including the shoeing of a team of oxen which were being used to pull a covered waggon round the countryside to advertise suet products. As for strength, Joe Price at the height of his powers could drive nails through a two-inch thick plank with his open palm. He could break building bricks lying on a flat surface by hitting them with his fist. He could strike a piece of metal with a hammer so hard and fast from cold that it became hot enough to light a cigarette. He would let a man clutch his hair and then swing him off the ground. He could hold two sturdy cart horses together while they struggled to break away. He could take a wooden road barrier in his teeth and swing it into the air. He could write his name on a blackboard with a weight of fifty-six pounds attached to his little finger. He would allow two strong men to wind a rope round his neck and let them do their best to strangle him. He would shape iron one inch wide and three-eighths thick into a design with his teeth, hands, legs and head.

He was a lifelong keep-fit man and gave shows all over the country to encourage an interest in exercise and body-building. At these shows he was known to take on a team of farm labourers at tug-of-war or to challenge all comers to lift with two hands a weight he could swing above his head with one.

In his youth he excelled at many sports and won medals for soccer and swimming. He played soccer several times for Swindon at half-back. He collected more than fifty medals and six cups for physical prowess and skill as a blacksmith. Among them were the British Amateur Weight-Lifting Championship of 1922-3, the World's Heavyweight Record Lift—430lb with the right hand and 406¾lb with the left hand, which were 'one hand dead lifts' in which a barbell is lifted from between the feet, the legs are straightened and the weight is held while the judge counts 'One, two'.

His awards for outstanding skill as a smith included the gold medal presented in 1928 by the Worshipful Company of Farriers of London to the British horse-shoeing champion, the medal given by the Royal Counties Agricultural Society for shoeing cart-horses and the medal for the Shoeing Championship of the Three Counties (Gloucestershire, Herefordshire and Worcestershire).

A mention can be made here of another sport which, originally at least, depended on the blacksmith. This is the sport of pitching horseshoes, which in America developed into a national sport: President Truman even had a horseshoe court at the White House. The sport did not become as popular in Britain, though at one time it was a common pastime in northern Ireland. In 1851, for example, the police in Belfast were forced to clear Old Lodge Road of horseshoe pitchers because several hundred of them were holding up the traffic with their play.

One of the few blacksmiths to have written his memoirs is Gaius Carley whose book, *The Memoirs of Gaius Carley, a Sussex Blacksmith*, was published in 1963 but written around 1953. He tells how he went to work at the age of fourteen at East Hoathly, a village near Lewes on the London—Eastbourne road, where the blacksmith was Johnnie Turner, a descendant of Turner the Diarist. It took Carley half an hour to walk to the smithy and he had to be there by six o'clock of a morning. A good deal of the trade came from the large horse-drawn vans

Children watch the smiths at work at the old blacksmith's shop at Tolleshunt d'Arcy, near Maldon, Essex

which were driven from London to the coast towns and were stabled overnight at the King's Arms in East Hoathly. Often these heavy horses needed shoeing before they started off in the morning.

Carley's first job was to keep the forge tidy and to learn the sizes of iron nuts and bolts, stocks and dies and the various tools. He had also to learn how to make different fires for different jobs.

At sixteen, Carley took a job at Blackboys (a village named after the old charcoal burners who at one time operated in the area), and here there were still oxen to be shod (by trussing and throwing on the ground). He only stayed a few weeks at Blackboys, however, moving on to Cobham forge belonging to blacksmith Turner at Edridge near Tunbridge Wells. That was in 1905. At Edridge there was not much shoeing but instead all sorts of jobs from the farms and hop fields. When the blacksmith wanted Carley's attention, he would 'tingle' the anvil with three sharp beats or rings. When he was making shoes and wanted harder blows from his mate he would give two strong beats on the anvil. For softer blows he would give one light beat. More speed was requested by three sharp beats, and a sudden bang down and stop meant cease sledging.

Among the many things Carley was called upon to do in his long life as a blacksmith were trimming cows' and goats' feet, mending children's toys and hoops, repairing prams and putting ferrules on walking sticks and wheelbarrows and, once, on a man's wooden leg!

Blacksmiths have even included an 'archbishop' in their ranks. This was Andrew Gladstone of the Scottish village of Yetholm in Roxburghshire, who succeeded his father as 'hereditary archbishop' of the Yetholm gipsies who had settled in the area several centuries before. One Whit Monday towards the close of the nineteenth century, Gladstone was called on to crown Charles Faa Blythe king of the Yetholm gipsies, for the reigning queen, Esther Fas Blythe, had died. The blacksmith read out a long proclamation which ended with the words 'Challenge who will'. This challenge was promptly taken up but was just as promptly dismissed, and Gladstone was next called on to perform the coronation ceremony.

Sleeves rolled up and wearing his leather apron, he took the crown (made of brass studded with imitation jewels) and in the

Romany tongue proclaimed:

As the Hereditary Archbishop of Yetholm I hereby crown Charles Faa Blythe as King of the Yetholm Gipsies, wherever they may be, and summon all his loyal people to do him respect and homage. Long live the King Charles!

The king then marched in procession through the village before escorting his consort to the 'Palace'—a little cottage.

One of the Yetholm gipsies was the model of Walter Scott's Meg Merrilees in *Guy Mannering*.

One of America's famous blacksmiths was Elihu Burritt, who was also an author and philanthropist. He was born at New Britain in Connecticut in 1810 where his father was shoemaker in winter and farmer in summer. As a youth Elihu showed a great thirst for knowledge but when his father died in 1828 he apprenticed himself to Samuel Booth the blacksmith in his native town—and blacksmith he remained one way or another in many different places for nearly twenty years.

Elihu was so keen on study that he took books to the smithy with him. One was James Thomson's *Seasons*, a book of romantic poetry, which he propped up against the forge chimney and, as the iron was heating and the sparks flying, 'took short sips of its beauty'.

When he was not reading, he occupied his mind with working out mathematical problems or learning a language. It is said that at the age of twenty-seven he could read in fifty languages.

But he suffered a breakdown in health and after a period of store-keeping and school-teaching he turned to lecturing. His main theme was international peace. In 1844 he started a paper called *The Christian Citizen*. In 1846 he sailed from Boston to England in the *Hibernia* and arrived in time to attend the final meeting of the Anti Corn-Law League at Manchester. The following year his *Sparks from the Anvil* was published by Charles Gilpin the philanthropic bookseller of Bishopsgate, London, followed by another volume *Voice from the Anvil*.

Elihu went to Ireland in the same year, when the potato famine was devastating the country, and he sent an appeal for aid to America. He did much work for the League of Universal Brotherhood and organised peace conferences at Brussels, Paris and Frankfurt-on-Main.

Returning to America he bought a small farm at New Britain and started a weekly national paper *North and South*, designed to advocate emancipation of the slaves by purchase, the expense to be defrayed by the sale of public lands. To get enough money for this project he lived for a while on eightpence a day, drinking nothing stronger than water.

In 1863 he went again to England and enjoyed a summer walk from London to John O'Groats, visiting on his way the chief agricultural establishments in the central and northern counties. The following year he walked from London to Land's End. In 1865 he was appointed United States consular agent at Birmingham, a post he held for four years. In 1870 at the age of sixty he returned to America.

A blacksmith who became a popular preacher was Samuel Hick of Micklefield near Aberford in Yorkshire. Born in 1758, one of a family of thirteen, he became apprentice to a blacksmith called Derby but was sacked for becoming too attached to the blacksmith's daughter. The daughter was fond of Samuel and used to give him gifts in the way of food and money. But one morning the blacksmith, on coming downstairs a little earlier than usual, found Samuel with Miss Derby on his knee. The blacksmith roused his wife, who was still in bed, saying, 'I believe she is as fond of the lad as ever a cow was of calf.' Going downstairs again he only scolded the couple, but he brooded about it all day and in the evening informed Samuel that he was dismissed. After Samuel had gone the daughter was quickly married off to another man, but she became very depressed and then insane and died soon afterwards.

A year or two later when Samuel had married another woman he was taken with religion. He composed two hymns and he preached a great deal, but only one of his sermons has been committed to writing. This was *Entire Sanctification,* which begins:

Naw, ye see ye've nobbut an oud Blacksmith in Pulpitt to neet, and soa ye noant ekspeckt a varree larn'd Sarmon; for ye see when I furst began to preitch I kud nother reed nor rite, an I'll uphod ya I wor soorlee freetend at I sud sa me Text rang; bud naw, bless the Lord, I can boath reed and rite.

Then follows a very long sermon.

A famous blacksmith of Wales was Dafydd y Gof, David Davies, who became an antiquary after teaching himself to read from sale bills and posters. He lived from 1822-91 and was a very skilled blacksmith said to be without equal in sharpening scythes, sickles and other tools.

Many other blacksmiths could be included in the category 'strange and strong', but in the main these men were a modest crowd, never seeking much publicity, and their names have been lost to posterity.

5

Blacksmith Priests of Gretna Green

'Oh, Mr Blacksmith, ease our pains
And tie us fast in wedlock's chains'
Caption to illustration in *The Gretna Blacksmith's Story*, 1928

The adaptable blacksmith was for a long time the forger not only
of ironware. A vivid picture of romance is conjured up by the
words 'blacksmith wedding' or 'blacksmith marriage', a term
which has been known since the fifteenth century and is thought
to be of continental origin. It seems to have been used originally
to cover all marriages where the ceremony was either non-
existent or of an unusual character.

In the *Diary of Mr Justice Rokeby*, 1693, there is an entry
from which it appears that a woman named Seager sued a
Mr Hopkins for damages for slander on the grounds that he had
proclaimed 'in market' that she was his wife by a 'blacksmith's
marriage' and had nailed up on the public pillory a statement to
that effect.

In Scotland, 'border marriages'—another term for the same
sort of thing—were taking place as early as 1639. The church
discipline in Scotland was so severe that many clergy would not

marry anyone who was not in full communion, and as a result many people went across to England and were married near the border by Episcopalian priests. But the marriages for English couples at Gretna in particular became popular after the Marriage Act of 1753, which was applicable only to England and which forbade marriages without previous banns being called. In Scotland, the old law of marriage by declaration in the presence of witnesses without any previous notice remained in force. It was Gretna Green, about ten miles north of Carlisle and situated on the main road out of England, that developed into the Mecca for clandestine weddings in the eighteenth and ninteenth centuries.

In 1750 the parish church at Gretna stood on the same site as today and along the road leading to the blacksmith's shop were just a few cottages and one large house. An inn faced the church on the opposite side of the green from which the village took its name. The present highway from Carlisle was merely a road for cattle and impassable to ordinary traffic. A few squatters lived on the outskirts of the green and there were some fishermen's rough huts and a small quay for their boats.

Gretna has had a chequered history. The whole of this border area was the scene of much fighting over several centuries, for in addition to the quarrels between the two kingdoms of England and Scotland many bitter fights took place among the border clans. In 1597 Kinmont Willie the border chieftain, after having failed to capture Carlisle from the English, was rescued from his captors and arrived at Gretna, where the village blacksmith removed his iron shackles for him. The last real fighting occurred when a detachment of Bonnie Prince Charlie's army went through the village in 1745. The Prince himself is said to have spent the night in a cottage opposite the smithy.

The village was in the possession of the Johnstone (Annondale) clan for several centuries. However, in the eighteenth century, about the time the marriages began, the landlord was an absentee and it was found difficult to lease the estate because

A nineteenth-century smithy, with stocks in the foreground. By
Birket Foster

of the threatening attitude of the villagers, notorious for their smuggling, which was carried out under the guise of fishing.

Much has been spoken and written about the 'blacksmith priests' of Gretna and about the wedding ceremonies performed in the 'blacksmith shop' but—in the main years at least—no true blacksmith seems to have been one of the priests and no one was married in a real smithy until 1907, when the village's genuine blacksmith shop was turned into a 'marriage house'. In fact, the art of farriery was little understood or practised in the border country at all until towards the end of the eighteenth century, when turnpike roads came into being and their hard surfaces made the shoeing of horses really necessary.

Yet by mid-eighteenth century Gretna was already famous. In 1783 a musical *Gretna Green* was produced at the Haymarket Theatre, London; it opened with a representation of a blacksmith's shop and it showed Gretna Green as a place of runaway marriages.

Though there was no real smithy in which to conduct the wedding ceremonies in the early days, this did not prevent the publicity material emanating from Gretna from depicting a blacksmith's shop; one of the earliest illustrations of a blacksmith marrying two people over an anvil appeared in 1792. The ceremony was simple and can be summed up in the nineteenth-century quatrain by Lord Charles Neaves:

Suppose young Jocky and Jenny
Say 'We two are husband and wife',
The witnesses needn't be many,
They're instantly buckled for life.

Joseph Paisley was one of the first and best-known of the Gretna Green priests. He was born in 1728 at the village of Lennoxton in the parish of Kirkandrews-on-Esk, Cumberland, the son of a dissenting clergyman. He was a fisherman and probably a smuggler under 'Auld Watty Coulthard', smuggler, fisherman and priest all in one at Sarkfoot, where he conducted weddings on the open beach. Paisley soon found he could conduct weddings as successfully as his master and he set up business on his own account at Gretna.

Paisley was a big, rough, hard-drinking Borderer who could bend a poker over his bare arms and straighten a horseshoe with his hands. For the last forty years of his life, he daily drank one Scots pint of straight brandy, which is equivalent to two and a quarter English pints. Once he and a bottle companion sat down to an anker (ten gallons) of strong cognac and after sixty hours of steady drinking kicked the empty cask to pieces for having run dry. And it was said that neither man was drunk! Paisley looked on whisky as the 'stuff women get drunk on'. His fee for marrying the well-to-do was £10 but he was quite willing to do the ceremony for poorer people in return for a bottle of brandy. Many clients crossed the Solway by ford or by boat; on one occasion a pursuing parent of a girl who came to Paisley to be married was drowned and Paisley's name became nationally known.

He grew enormously fat and at one time weighed over twenty-five stone. In his old age he was very coarse in his manners but he lived until he was eighty-four when he was buried in Gretna Green churchyard.

Coulthard, Paisley's early master, himself moved to Gretna Green when he saw the amount of business that was possible there. He married his customers from an ale-house close to where Paisley operated.

One of these 'priests' probably married the famous John Peel when he ran away with Mary White. The couple had had their banns proclaimed in Cauldbeck parish church but Mary's mother had objected to the marriage, saying that her daughter was too young. So Mary climbed out of her bedroom window and went with her lover to Gretna Green. The wedding was the theme of a contemporary song.

After the wedding the couple rode back to Cauldbeck where a loud 'View halloa' from John Peel announced to the wife's

A Country Blacksmith Disputing upon the Price of Iron, by J. M. W. Turner, about 1800

parents and to all the villagers that the couple were married. Later, however, they had a proper ceremony in the parish church.

Through all the popular literature on Gretna Green runs this idea of a blacksmith shop where people were married.

> *But we stood at the Blacksmith's door at last,*
> *And he forged in the glimmering moonlight sheen*
> *A fetter of silver to bind us fast,*
> *Lover to lover, at Gretna Green.*

David Lang, the son of a sister of Joseph Paisley, was a pedlar and then a sailor, and at one period a pirate. At the age of thirty-eight he slipped away from his ship and came back to Gretna, where he set up as priest in opposition to his uncle and to the others, who now included Robert Elliott and Tom Little. He was succeeded in 1821 by his son Simon, who in turn was followed in 1872 by his son William, by which time trade had declined so much that William had to act also as village postman in order to make a living.

Robert Elliott, the son of a farmer, was born at Galashiels Rigg, in Northumberland. He went in for stable work and on marrying Anne Graham, a granddaughter of Joseph Paisley, he came to live at Gretna. They stayed at Paisley's alehouse and when Paisley grew old Elliott took over his business.

Tom Little, known as the 'Piper', was working on the English side of the border before he got into trouble and fled to Scotland, taking refuge at Gretna. He saw the possibilities in the growing number of runaway marriages and set up on his own as a 'priest' at the Queen's Head. On his door was a picture of a blacksmith with hammer upraised over the clasped hands of a pair of lovers.

One of the best-known priests in the early years of the twentieth century was Tom Johnstone, who was conspicuous in that he always wore a frock coat and top hat for his weddings, and made his visits in one of the early motor cars.

So many 'priests' eventually set up at Gretna that the slight dignity which had once been bestowed upon the trade was

Gretna Green blacksmith's shop, with priest Tom Johnstone, early twentieth century, on his first motor-car run

completely lost and disgraceful scenes of scrambling and snatching at potential customers took place. As soon as a couple alighted from a coach they were besieged by touts, and when the railway was built things grew so bad that the station-master was forced to make the 'priests' stand in line behind the railway station while the customers from the train made their own selection. All the 'priests' dressed in white and kept grave faces.

John Linton, who started officiating in 1825, used the fairly grand Gretna Hall, which had once been a coaching inn, for his weddings and specialised in aristocratic affairs. Maybe one of his weddings inspired the Mother Goose rhyme:

Once in my life I married a wife
And where do you think I found her?
On Gretna Green, in a velvet sheen,
And I took up a stick to pound her.
She jumped over a barberry bush
And I jumped over a timber,
I showed her a gay, gold ring
And she showed me her finger.

By the eighteen-seventies the people of Gretna were so disgusted at the things going on in their village that when people came demanding to see the 'blacksmith's shop' they were inclined to deny its existence.

In 1907 the real village smithy was converted into a shop for the sale of curios and as a place where the ceremonies could take place. Now it was a proper blacksmith-shop wedding. One of the curios was the anvil reputed to be 400 years old. But the locals said that this had been bought new in the second half of the nineteenth century by Harkness the real blacksmith of Gretna, who had never been connected with the marrying. Harkness himself had given up blacksmithing in Gretna and had gone off to Carlisle, taking his anvil with him. But his son sold it back to Gretna.

People from many countries were married at Gretna—the

registers had entries from France, Belgium, Holland, Germany, America and elsewhere.

In 1927 Dick Rennison was employed by Hugh Mackie, the Laird of Gretna, to marry runaway couples in the real black-smith's shop. He officiated at 5,147 weddings up to 1940, when at long last these ceremonies were declared illegal.

These blacksmith weddings led to much doubt in later years as to the authenticity of some of the marriages. In 1924, for example, a worried German wrote from Wilhelmshaven:

Mr Possessor
of the Smithery (Justice of the Peace)
at Gretna Green,
County Dumfries, Scotland (Great Britain)
    Knowing that many young persons have been copulated in your old historical Smithery, I beg your pardon because I find it necessary to inform me whether my father in travelling to the U.S.A. has been with his bride in Gretna Green in the year 1845 or 1844 or 1846.
    My letter relates to an inheritance where I must possess a certificate of marriage with regard to my deceased father. After having written to many authorities of my country I don't believe that this marriage has taken place here.
    The name of my father was Johannes Voller, born the 2nd of May 1811 at Altenburg (Aberhessen), of his bride Ulrike Wilhelmine Gretsel or Grettel, born the 29th of January in 1808 at Sorau (Niederlausitz). It is not impossible that they have gone away together before continuing their way at first over Hull to Gretna Green, and you would render me a very great service to look in your book for these names.
    At each case I beg you very cordially to answer as soon as possible, also in case that my father's and his bride's names would not be in your books.
    You will take in advance the heartiest thanks of an old, poor man to whom, by this inheritance, a possibility is

KINGDOM OF SCOTLAND.

COUNTY OF DUMFRIES.

PARISH OF GRETNA.

· · ·

These are to Certify to all whom they may
concern : That..... *Michael Joseph Wyne*
from the Parish of.....
in the County of..... *London*
and ..... *Marguerite Marchmont*
from the Parish of.... *Mount Florida*
in the County of..... *Glasgow*
being now both here present, and having declared to me
that they are Single Persons, have now been Married
after the manner of the Laws of Scotland : As witness
our hands at Gretna, this **28**th
day of *Feb 1920*.....

Parties { *Michael Joseph Wyne*
Margaretete Marchmont
R Nugent

Witnesses { *Mary Hough*
Priest *R Nugent*

Gretna Green marriage certificate of 1920

found for a careless evening of life. As soon as I am in
possession of this inheritance it shall be a duty to me to
show me grateful over against you.

I am, your very respectful

G. Voller, Master Tailor

The genuine blacksmiths in both Scotland and England were naturally not very pleased at the bad name that Gretna gave to their profession. There was not much they could do about it, but on one occasion they had a chance to show their disapproval. This was in Dick Rennison's time when this 'anvil priest' was invited to the annual dinner of the Birmingham Blacksmiths Association. Several members objected to his being invited and said that they did not like to see the honourable trade of black-smiths 'trailed in the mud by carrying-on that would-be marriage ceremony at Gretna and causing untold misery to many poor girls who are led away with the glamour of the place . . .'

In 1969 Dick Rennison, the last of the 'blacksmith priests', died at the age of seventy-six at his home in Cumberland.

6

The
Spreading Chestnut Tree

'It has always struck me that there is something highly poetical about a forge'

George Borrow: *Lavengro*, 1851

Longfellow's *The Village Blacksmith* did much to boost the morale of the blacksmith from the middle of the nineteenth century onwards. Until this poem spread through the English-speaking world the blacksmith had in general been a poorly paid, rather shy man. Longfellow persuaded him that he was honest— 'His brow is wet with honest sweat'; strong—'The muscles of his brawny arms Are strong as iron bands'; and respectable—'He looks the whole world in the face, For he owes not any man'.

Henry Wadsworth Longfellow, born in 1807, was an American, though many British blacksmiths believed—and still, in fact, do —that he was English and was writing about them. But he did have English ancestors. A William Longfellow emigrated to New England in 1660 and married Ann Sewall, another English settler, in 1676. William is mentioned in the 'List of Grantees and Genealogy of the First Settlers of the Town of Newbury in Essex County, Massachusetts', where it is stated that he was

born in Hampshire. But the poet Longfellow always maintained that his family came from Calverley near Pudney in Yorkshire. Possibly he was descended from James Langfellay of Otlay in Yorkshire who lived around 1450. James was followed by the Rev Sir Peter Langfellowe but then in the genealogical table three generations are missing until an Edward Longfellow appears in 1590. The William Longfellow who emigrated to Newbury, Massachusetts, at the age of ten was probably born in Hampshire in 1650 but moved north to Yorkshire at an early age, possibly because of the break-up of the clothing industry in the south due to the Civil War. The Longfellows were clothiers. The Sewall family he married into came from Coventry.

The town of Newbury in Massachusetts was founded by the Rev Thomas Parker (assistant to Dr Twiss, the Puritan Rector of Newbury in Berkshire, Prolocutor of the Westminster Assembly of Divines) and a party of co-religionists who in 1634 gave the name of Newbury to the new settlement in honour of their first pastor Thomas Parker.

Another theory is that the name Longfellow stems from the Norman family name of Longvillers. At Laxton Church in Nottinghamshire a stained-glass window bears the arms of the Longvillers—'sable, a bend between six cross-crosslets arg.' In 1530 a Peter Langefelowe, clerk, was one of the original trustees of Magnus's Charity at Newark-on-Trent which is in Nottinghamshire. And there was a Jo Longfelow who was of the household of Sir Thomas Wentworth (afterwards Earl of Strafford) about 1615-20.

Henry Longfellow the poet became a teacher and spent eight years at Bowdoin College and eighteen years at Harvard. In 1836 his first wife died and seven years later he married Elizabeth Appleton and went to live at Cambridge in Massachusetts. He died in 1882 and two years later his bust was placed in the Poets' Corner of Westminster Abbey, for his fame was almost as truly British as American.

It is almost certain that it was the blacksmith shop at Cambridge in Massachusetts that Longfellow wrote about in *The Village Blacksmith*, though there are quite a few claims to the contrary. The name of the smith was Dexter Pratt and his smithy stood on the west side of Brattle Street between Story Street and Farwell Place. The poet passed the smithy daily on his way to Harvard College and often paused to watch the blacksmith at work. Pratt carried on the shop from 1829 to about 1840. He died on 4 October 1847 at the age of forty-six and was buried in Mount Auburn Cemetery, Cambridge. His house in Brattle Street still stands, but the 'spreading chestnut tree' was cut down in 1875 so that the street could be widened. The figure of Pratt is among those represented in low relief on the Longfellow memorial in Longfellow Park, Cambridge.

In 1840 Longfellow wrote to his father, 'I have written a kind of ballad on a blacksmith. A song of praise to our ancestor

'The smith, a mighty man.' This illustration appeared in an early edition of Longfellow's poems, and it may show the original smith of *The Village Blacksmith*

of Newbury.' The poem was first published in *The Knicker-bocker Magazine* of New York, November 1840. It is given in full in the Appendix on pages 152-3.

When the chestnut tree was cut down Professor and Mrs E. N. Horsford saved some of the wood and had it made into a chair finished in imitation of ebony to a design by W. P. P. Long-fellow, the poet's nephew. It was presented to the poet by schoolchildren on his birthday, 27 February 1879.

The fact that Longfellow allowed himself to be presented with this chair would seem to settle the question of whether the Cambridge smithy was the inspiration of *The Village Blacksmith*. He also wrote a poem *From my Arm-Chair*, which he dedicated to the children of Cambridge 'who presented to me, on my Seventy-Second Birthday, this chair made from the Wood of the Village Blacksmith's Chestnut Tree'.

Am I a King, that I should call my own
This splendid ebon throne?
Or by what reason, or what right divine,
Can I proclaim it my own?

Only, perhaps, by right divine of song
It may to me belong;
Only because the spreading chestnut tree
Of old was sung by me.

Later the poet adds:

I see the smithy with its fires aglow,
I hear the bellows blow,
And the shrill hammer on the anvil beat
The iron white with heat.

But despite this, there were claims by other blacksmiths who thought they had been Longfellow's source of inspiration. Another blacksmith at Cambridge, Massachusetts, was Thadeus W. Tyler, who late in life lived at Lynn near Boston, where he often

spoke of his acquaintance with the poet and said that Longfellow had showed him the manuscript of *The Village Blacksmith* before it was published.

Blacksmith Henry Francis Moore of Medford in Massachusetts claimed that Longfellow was often in Medford previous to
the publication of his poem and was fond of chatting to him.
Moore was certain that Longfellow had him in mind when he
wrote the poem. But as Moore was in his teens at the time
the poem was written, it would not seem likely that Longfellow
would write about this man's 'brawny arms' or 'listening to his
daughter's voice, Singing in the village choir'.

More than likely Longfellow had several smithies in his recollection when he wrote his poem; and an English smithy
could have been among them, for he knew England well. At the
village of Calverley near Pudney in Yorkshire—a village which
he spoke of as being the home of his ancestors and which he
visited on several occasions—there was a smithy complete with

Blacksmith at Staveley, near Kendal in Westmorland, about 1880

chestnut tree. At Dunchurch in Warwickshire was another smithy which laid claim to being the original of the poem: at one time a map under the portico of the Pump Room at Leamington Spa showed interesting places to visit and described Dunchurch as the 'Origin of Longfellow's *Village Blacksmith*' —though the chestnut tree growing there would seem to have been too young to have existed in Longfellow's time.

Probably his poems dealing with blacksmiths (and there were several) contained both American and British memories. The subject fascinated him, and the blacksmith appears particularly in *Nuremberg* and *Evangeline*. The most welcome suitor of Evangeline is Gabriel Lajeunnesse, the son of Basil the blacksmith. Basil is a friend of Benedict Bellefontaine the farmer and their children grow up together. There is an account of a visit to the smithy by these children when they come out of school:

Swiftly they hurried away to the forge of Basil the blacksmith.
There at the door they stood, with wondering eyes to behold him
Take in his leathern lap the hoof of the horse as a plaything,
Nailing the shoe in its place; while near him the tire of the cartwheel
Lay like a fiery snake, coiled around on a circle of cinders.
Oft on autumnal eves, when without in the gathering darkness
Bursting with light seemed the smithy through every cranny and crevice,
Warm by the forge within they watched the labouring bellows
And as its panting ceased, and the sparks expired in the ashes
Merrily laughed . . .

Longfellow of course was not the only man to write about the blacksmith, who has been a subject for poetry and song throughout the ages. The Bible describes him in Isaiah 44 v 12:

> *The smith with the tongs both worketh in the coals, and*
> *fashioneth it with hammers, and worketh it with the strength*
> *of his arms . . .*

And again in Isaiah 54 v 16:

> *Behold, I have created the smith that bloweth the coals in*
> *the fire, and that bringeth forth an instrument for his*
> *work . . .*

And Ecclesiasticus 38 v 28 on has an account of 'the smith also sitting by the anvil'.

In the sixteenth century Edmund Spenser mentioned the smith in a poem. An 'Ode on Smithery 1610' was published in Hone's *Every-Day Book* of 1830. Shakespeare speaks of a rather credulous smith in *King John*, Act IV Scene 2:

> *I saw a Smith stand with his hammer, thus*
> *The whilst his iron did on the anvil cool,*
> *With open mouth swallowing a Tailor's news . . .*

In the seventeenth century there was a famous song called *The Blacksmith*. Samuel Pepys writes in his *Diary* for 24 April 1660: 'William Howe and I went to play two trebles in the Great Cabin below, when my Lord hearing, after supper he called for our instruments and played, and then he fell to singing of a song made upon the rump to the tune of *The Blacksmith*'. The tune seems to have been the same as *Greensleeves*.

The folk song *Twankydillo* has already been mentioned, but the most famous piece of music written about the blacksmith is probably Handel's *The Harmonious Blacksmith*. The name was given to the air on which Handel wrote variations in his *Suite in E major* published in 1720. The story is that Handel took refuge in a blacksmith's shop at Edgware, Middlesex, during a storm and that the blacksmith, one Powell, sang the song as he hammered on the anvil. But this story did not become current

A blacksmith of nearly eighty still at work in his forge at Merton, Surrey in 1960. By then there were few horses in the area but he was kept busy repairing tools and plant for local factories until 1835 and the name of Powell was not mentioned until later still, when the anvil was mysteriously 'discovered' and sold by auction. By the end of the eighteenth century however the title had become established, for the publishers J. & W. Lintern brought out an edition under that name.

Another version is that Handel obtained his inspiration from a blacksmith near Tunstall, Newcastle-under-Lyme, when he was staying at Turnhurst Hall.

Longfellow's poem was turned into a platform song by Weiss. Other musical items are Mozart's *Oh! the blacksmith's a fine sturdy fellow*, and Brahms's *The Blacksmith I hear* and *The Blacksmith's Sweetheart*.

George Borrow was a writer who had much to do with blacksmiths though they were mostly gipsies. In *Lavengro* he writes of the smith's forge:

> *I love to light upon such a one, especially after nightfall, as everything about a forge tells to the most advantage at night, the hammer sounds more solemnly in the stillness; the glowing particles scattered by the strokes sparkle with more effect in the darkness, whilst the sooty visage of the sastramescro, half in shadow and half illumined by the red and partial blaze of the forge, looks more mysterious and strange . . .*

There is a story about Coleridge stopping at a Somerset smithy to have a shoe replaced on his horse. While there he asked the blacksmith the time. The blacksmith bent down, lifted up one of the horse's hind legs and, seeming to gaze fixedly at it, said, 'Half-past eleven.' Coleridge was naturally astonished and asked the blacksmith how he knew so accurately by inspecting the leg of a horse. The blacksmith replied with a smile, 'Do you think, sir, that I have shod horses all my life and don't know by the sign what the time is?'

Coleridge puzzled over the matter for some time but could think of no explanation, so finally he asked for one. The smith

The Morning's Gossip from the *Farriers' Annual*, 1911. 'Strong arm
wanted—will I do?' The symbol of the blacksmith's strong arm hangs
down beside the chain. The smith is wearing the typical fringed apron

smiled again and replied, 'Come here, sir. Now stoop down and look past the horses hind leg to that pollarded oak yonder.' Coleridge did so. Through a gap in the branches of the oak tree the church clock was plainly visible.

The blacksmith himself by the very nature of his work was susceptible to poetry and often made an attempt to break into verse, even in his trade journals. Often these attempts were just parodies of *The Village Blacksmith*. But one J. H. could write in February 1929 when King George v was seriously ill:

When in my forge, my head I bare
And bow it down in silent prayer
For our beloved King,
I pray that God who rules above
Will in his mercy and his love
Our King to us restore.

But to go back to Longfellow. An American school-teacher was talking to her class before studying *The Village Blacksmith*. She said to them, 'Now, children, we are going to learn a poem today about someone who works very hard. He is very large, and has great arms that can lift very heavy things. His face is blackened with soot that comes from the fire. He wears a dirty, black apron, and he has a fire that glows red, and whenever he makes anything he puts it into his fire, then pounds it with a great hammer, which makes a clanging noise and makes the sparks fly all about. Now, who can tell me what I have been describing?'

A little girl replied in an awed whisper, 'The Devil!'

7

Horseshoes as Charms

'See a horseshoe, pick it up
And all the year you'll have good luck'
Old saying

Iron, and particularly the horseshoe, has been recognised as an emblem against spirits since very early days. One example of this is the story in chapter 1 of Saint Dunstan exacting a promise from the Devil that he would not enter a building where a horseshoe was displayed.

Witches, wizards, ogres, gnomes, fairies, ghosts, trolls, pixies, elves, leprechauns, goblins and all kinds of other demons and spirits and 'little people' at one time formed an important part of man's life and lived their own lives alongside that of humans. It is only in comparatively recent times that they have been pushed out of everyday existence.

Some of these supernatural and mythological beings were helpful to mankind; others could be extremely antagonistic and ready to do harm at any opportunity. Against the malevolent ones protection was always needed, while even the friendly ones required to be shown gratitude from time to time—or they were inclined to become peevish. So from childhood to old age early man had to ward off or placate these other beings who occupied the earth with him. Charms were employed as a protection against the evil spirits and iron, from the time of its first discovery, was a major charm.

For example, one of the dangers to a newly born child was that the fairies, not with evil intent but purely out of mischief, would take it and put an elf-child in its place. But their plans could be thwarted if a piece of iron and the father's coat were put at the foot of the bed where the mother and child were sleeping. If the child was on its own in a cradle a pair of scissors or a knife placed nearby would do.

Three circles drawn with an iron weapon in the air round a person, and three on the ground enclosing his feet, were a proven protection against witchcraft; nails driven into a house would keep out the plague. In Roman times wedding rings were sometimes made of iron. Iron buried beneath an ash tree would give the tree power the following spring to cure cows which were suffering from the 'evil eye'.

The most popular form of using iron as a charm, however, was the horseshoe. Cast shoes were quite easy to find and soon there arose the custom of nailing a horseshoe to a door to keep away evil spirits or to avoid bad luck. John Brooks Felton spoke of this protection in 1849 in his poem *The Horse-shoe*.

Oft have I heard them chattering at my door,
The hags whose dances beat the shrinking moor;
Oft have I sprung from night-mare haunted rest,
And gasped an oro from my panting breast,
As forms that vanished ere the half-shut eye
With fright could open, from their revels fly,
Henceforth, good horse-shoe, vain shall be their ride:
Their spells are baffled, and their rage defied.

It is a custom still ranging over much of the world. At one time in England nearly every country cottage and farmhouse had a

The famous old smithy of Claverdon in Warwickshire, where the door frame is reputed to be the largest horseshoe in the world

horseshoe nailed above its door. Aubrey, in his *Miscellanies* in 1696, said that most houses in the west end of London had the horseshoe on the threshold; in Monmouth Street seventeen were counted in 1813, and still seven as late as 1855. And around the same period, Whittier says in *The Witch's Daughter*:

And still o'er many a neighbouring door
She saw the horse-shoe's curvéd charm.

Sometimes an enlarged horseshoe even became the door frame or the entrance to the forge. An old smithy at Claverdon, Warwickshire, has a doorway which is said to be made of the largest horseshoe in the world. Horseshoes were often nailed to the west doors of churches. There used to be two horseshoes on the door of the parish church of Haccombe in Devonshire. An old ballad describes how, for a wager, the Earl of Totnes on a

Devonshire roan raced against Sir Arthur Champernowne on a Barbary courser. The Earl won and from the winning post rode straightway to Haccombe church, where he nailed the roan's shoes to the door.

At Stanfield church in Suffolk in the seventeenth century there was a tile with a horseshoe in it. Aubrey says it was placed there to keep out witches, 'though one would imagine that holy-water would alone have been sufficient'.

In Gay's fable *The Old Woman and the Cat* the old woman complains:

> *Crowds of boys*
> *Worry me with eternal noise;*
> *Straws laid across my pace retard*
> *The horse-shoes nail'd (each threshold's guard).*

And in Scott's *Redgauntlet*, Summertrees says to Crosbie, 'Your wife's a witch, man; you should nail a horse-shoe on your chamber-door.'

Although the iron itself was a powerful charm, horseshoes were also thought to perplex witches trying to get into a building. The witch would mistake the shoe for a circle and would start to go round it. But the ends puzzled her and she kept travelling from one end to the other until sunrise when, as witches always did, she had to flee.

In the *London World* of August 1753 an article dealing with the repeal of the so-called Witches Act said satirically:

> *To secure yourself against the enchantment of witches,*
> *especially if you are a person of fashion and have never been*
> *taught the Lord's Prayer, the only method I know of is to*
> *nail a horse-shoe upon the threshold. This I can affirm to be*
> *of the greatest efficacy, insomuch that I have taken notice*
> *of many a little cottage in the country with a horse-shoe at*
> *its door where gaming, extravagance, Jacobitism and all the*
> *catalogue of witchcrafts have been totally unknown.*

The Forge, by Joseph Wright, 1771

An old book of charms laid down that if a horse were shod with shoes made from a sword with which a man had been slain it would be swift and never tire.

Perhaps the lucky quality of horseshoes was handed down from Hecate the moon goddess, who wore a crescent and seven stars on her head. Diana in her character of Hecate was ruler of the infernal regions and presided over enchantment, and was also the special guardian of houses and doors.

The use of a horseshoe for good luck at a wedding is said to date from the time of Lars Porsena, King of the Tuscans, whose queen had her horse shod in silver on her marriage day.

From other countries come other stories. Pliny said that if someone found a cast shoe he should remember the exact spot, and at any time afterwards that he suffered from hiccoughs the recollection of that spot would cure them. In Ceylon the shape of the horseshoe is said to resemble the arched body of the sacred snake Nagendra, one of the principal gods, and so the horseshoe is sacred itself. To the Turks it is a crescent—the sacred emblem of Islam. In Hindu temples it is a phallic symbol representing the 'yoni'. Polish Jews say it is the shape in which they have always sprinkled blood at the Passover. In Italy in the Middle Ages it was the custom to put a crescent-shaped hood of brass on the statues of saints exposed in the open as a protection against rain and snow: later images in churches were adorned in this fashion and horseshoes became a cheap substitute.

In the Caucasus the peasant hallowed the horseshoe because it was the means by which their ancestors had first learnt the use of iron. According to legend some poor peasants found a shoe that had been thrown from the horse of a Cossack chieftain. They had never seen anything made from iron before. They tried to cook and eat it and then they beat it. Satan, who was standing by watching, asked what they were doing and they told him they were making a hammer to beat him with. 'But,' said Satan, 'you have no sand.' And so they learnt that sand was essential to the making of iron.

Ireland may once have been Ironland. Legend has it that the country was once submerged in the sea from whence it arose only once every seven years. Many attempts were made to break what was a spell and to keep the land permanently above water. But all were in vain until one day a man threw a horse-shoe from a boat on to the topmost peak of the Wicklow mountains just as they were disappearing beneath the waves. The power of the iron was great enough to overcome the power of the spell: Ireland rose from the waters and never went below again.

In the central Arabian desert cast horseshoes were preserved in a goatskin bag together with seven nails. The bag was worn round the neck as a charm when an Arab was out riding or was suspended over the entrance to his quarters when he was resting. The Tuscan peasant substituted seven glass beads for the seven nails and made the bag of red cloth.

In Thuringia in Germany, horseshoes were not lucky unless

Smithy at Lealholm Hall, near Whitby, Yorkshire, about 1880

they had been forged on St John's Eve in a certain spot in the middle of the street by a young bachelor of wholesome life. In Prussia two large horseshoes used to hang on a church wall near Rastenburg and there was a story concerning them. Near the church lived an innkeeper who did not give correct measure. One night the Devil came in and, changing the innkeeper into a horse, took him to the village blacksmith and said, 'Master, shoe my horse.' The blacksmith was about to do so when the horse whispered in his ear, 'Work slowly.' Hearing the horse speak, the blacksmith was so frightened and trembled so much that he did take a long time, and he had not got very far before the cock crew and the Devil was obliged to leave. At this the innkeeper regained his shape, but he was very ill for a long time.

When a blacksmith of the German Tyrol ceased work on a Saturday evening he would strike three blows upon the anvil with his hammer, in order that the Devil should be chained up for the ensuing week. Likewise, while hammering a horseshoe into shape, the smith would strike the anvil instead of the shoes with every fourth or fifth blow and would thus make doubly secure the chain with which the Devil was bound.

At Ellrich in Germany four huge shoes were nailed to the door of the church as a reminder of the fate of a Count Ernest, who one Sunday morning rode from Kletternberg to Ellrich to take part in a drinking competition for a chain of gold. He won, and putting the chain round his neck he rode through Ellrich to Kletternberg. Vespers were being said in the church of St Nicholas as he passed through the town square and he rode in over the people right to the altar. But the moment the horse put its feet on the altar its four shoes were torn off and it fell, with its rider, dead on the floor.

The plant moon-wort (*Botrychium lunaria*) also had the reputation for drawing the shoes off horses' feet; and it was said to be able to do this because of the crescent form of the fern segments. In the sixteenth century Du Bartas wrote:

And horse that, feeding on the grassy hills,
Tread upon moon-wort with their hollow heeles,
Though lately shod, at night goe bare-foot home,
Their master musing where their shoes be gone.

Culpepper refers to the same belief. He tells of the time when the Earl of Essex had his cavalry drawn up in a body on White Down near Tiverton in Devon, and when many of the horses lost their shoes from the moon-wort growing there. Moon-wort also had the reputation of being able to open the locks of dwelling-houses if placed in the keyhole.

Horseshoes were accepted as a charm or as a protection against evil spirits from a very early time. But which way up should one hang the shoe to be most effective? There are two schools of thought on this: one says that the points must be upward to keep the luck from running out, and the other that they should be downwards so that the luck can run out on to the house or on to work being done. To be on the safe side some people hang up two horseshoes, one each way. But ancient custom seems to have been to face the points downwards— old blacksmiths would hang a shoe downwards over their hearth

The smithy and the White Lion Inn at Ambleside, Westmorland, in 1825

to let the luck run out on to it. Walter Marshall, seventh Earl of Pembroke, who died in 1246, had for his seal a horseshoe with the points downward. The ancient seal of the City of Gloucester bears two horseshoes similarly placed, and the horseshoes in the Rutland coat of arms also have their points facing downward (page 19).

The Gloucester mayoral chain is made of horseshoes and these pointed downward until in 1930 the mayor had them changed so that the luck could not run out. He claimed as a result such benefits as being able to introduce a rate reduction of tenpence in the pound. But the next mayor had the shoes put back the original way, as he maintained that unemployment during his predecessor's time had been a record high!

A pleasant custom was for a girl to count the number of empty nail holes in a cast-off shoe—it indicated the number of years she must wait to get married.

There is an old German spell for the protection of a horse's hoof when a shoe is lost:

Take a bread-knife and cut the hoof at the edge . . . and lay the knife crosswise on the sole and say, 'I command thee, hoof and horn, that thou breakest as little as God the Lord broke his word, when he created heaven and earth.' And thou shalt say these words three hours in succession and five Paternosters and five Ave Marias to the praise of the Virgin. Then the horse will not walk lame until thou happenest to reach a smithy.

There is also a German saying with regard to a young girl who has been led astray: 'She has lost a horseshoe.'

Just as luck was connected with a horseshoe, so many superstitions arose also over the blacksmith and his work. Warts, for example, could be cured by dipping one's hand in the water of a blacksmith's trough after any horse had been shod on three feet. Trough water was also good for bathing wounds.

For goitre it was necessary to inhale the smoke from the hoof

Blacksmith's forge in the mid nineteenth century. From *Scenes of Commerce*, by the Reverend Isaac Taylor, 1845

of an ass which had never been in foal, and as soon as possible after she had lost one of her shoes.

An ailing child could be cured if he was stripped naked and laid on the anvil, his mother holding one arm, another woman holding both his feet and the blacksmith placing his left hand under the child's neck. Then the smith would bring his hammer down with a tremendous blow on the horn of the anvil, causing the child's body almost to spring from it. This was supposed to drive the sickness out!

In Scotland it was claimed that a child could be cured of rickets if he were bathed in the smithy trough and then laid on the anvil with iron implements passed over him, and if the ceremony ended with another bath. But there was a proviso that three blacksmiths of the same name had to take part in the ceremony, so it could not have occurred very often.

Another method, which must have been even more rarely used, was to bring the sick child to a blacksmith of the seventh generation and put him on the anvil. The smith would let his hammer fall gently three times on the child's body.

Walter Scott relates in *Lockhart's Life* how he found a man he had known as a blacksmith in Scotland practising as a qualified doctor in Northumberland. The man, John Lundie, told Scott that he relied on two simples, 'laudamy and calamy', and that his practice was 'verra sure and orthodox'. Asked if he had ever killed a patient he replied, 'Ou, ay, may be sae. Whiles they die, and whiles no; but it's the will of Providence. Onyhow, your honour, it wad be lang before it makes up for Flodden.'

In Galloway, Scotland, there used to be a blacksmith to whom barefoot children would go in winter with chilblains which he touched with a red-hot awl heated in the smithy fire. Up until recent days many blacksmiths would touch a wound or skin eruption with a piece of iron to cure it. It may have been something in the iron that effected the cure for even today doctors prescribe iron tonics. The Romans attempted to cure chest complaints by pricking the skin with the point of an iron weapon that had wounded a man.

In the sixteenth century there was a devastating outbreak of cattle disease in France. The church key which had been made by the local blacksmith was heated red-hot and applied to the foreheads of healthy animals as a prophylactic.

Many blacksmiths would never work on Good Friday, no matter whose horse had cast a shoe, for they were convinced that the Devil would have them if they did. The basis of this fear was the memory of the Crucifixion when nails were used so wickedly. The blacksmiths thought it sacrilege to touch nails on the anniversary of that date.

Many horse complaints were thought to be caused by evil spirits. The old 'Horseman' societies had closely guarded cures, charms, protective amulets and so on. They also possessed (and zealously guarded) a password or word of power known in

Scotland as the 'Horseman's Word' and in England as the 'Whisper', by which fractious and vicious horses could be rendered docile.

Elf-shot was a common trouble with horses in ancient times and was said to have been caused by the horse being shot by an elf-arrow, which was a neolithic flint. An Anglo-Saxon collection of leechdoms, remedies and recipes entitled *Lacnunga* says:

> *If a horse be elf-shot, then take the knife of which the haft is horn of a fallow ox, and one which be three brass nails, then write upon the horse's forehead Christ's mark and on each of the limbs, which thou may feel at: then take the left ear, prick a hole in it in silence, this thou shalt do; then take a yard, stroke the horse on the back, then will it be whole, and write upon the horn of the knife these words, 'Benedicite omnia opera domini dominum', Be the elf what it may this is mighty for him to amend.*

Horse nightmares were thought to be caused by a wicked hag or ogress named Mara, who took horses and rode them hard throughout the night, with the result that in the morning the horses would be dripping with sweat and their manes would be tangled. But iron could keep Mara out:

> *Hang up Hooks and Sheers, to scare*
> *Hence the Hag that rides the mare . . .*

Horses could suffer from many troubles and it was up to the blacksmith, before the advent of the veterinary surgeon, to know how to put the matter right. In *The Taming of the Shrew* Shakespeare gives some idea of what diseases a horse could suffer when Biondello speaks of Petruchio riding on one that was afflicted with a variety of ailments:

> *. . . possess'd with the glanders, and like to mose in the chine, troubled with the lampass, infected with the fashions, full of windgalls, sped with spavins, ray'd with the yellows,*

Visit to a horse doctor in the eighteenth century. From *A Practical Treatise on Farriery*, 1784, by William Griffiths

*past cure of the fives, stark spoiled with staggers, be-
gnawn with the bots, sway'd in the back . . .*

Lampass or lampas was generally defined as a swelling behind
the teeth and it made a horse listless. It is now thought to be
inflammation of the gums brought about by indigestion. The
early blacksmiths claimed to be able to cure it by burning the
mouth of the horse with a red-hot iron. In 1810 Francis Clater
(in his *Everyman his own Farrier*) described lampas as

*. . . an excrescence on the first bar in the roof of the horse's
mouth. The cure is generally performed by burning it out
with a hot iron; but it requires care, and a man of judgement, to perform operations of this kind. Farriers, in general,
are too apt to take out more than is necessary; care, however, must be taken not to burn out more than the first bar
in the roof of the mouth, and not too deep. Afterwards rub
his mouth, or the part seared, with common salt. It would
be much better for the animal to omit burning them out,
and to wash his mouth once or twice a day with the following mixture.*

    Take—Nitre, half an ounce;
        *Burnt alum, and bole armenic, in powder, of each
        one ounce;*
        Honey, two ounces:
*Put them in a pitcher, and then pour a pint of boiling
vinegar upon them; when cold, put them in a bottle for
use.*

*The mouth must be washed with this mixture once or
twice a day, which may be done by fastening a linen rag
round the end of a stick, dipping it in the mixture, and
introducing it into his mouth. This will take away the sore-
ness and harden his mouth, from which there will be no
necessity to remove the lampas by actual cautery.*

As late as 1914 this burning was still practised. At Enfield
in Middlesex in that year David Hale, a farmer, and Percy

Manning, a blacksmith, were summonsed for burning the mouth
of a horse. The burns were over three inches across, said a
veterinary surgeon called as expert witness, and all that the horse
was suffering from was inflammation of the gums which lotions
would have cured. But the blacksmith said, 'I have fired thousands, and I hope to fire many more.' He was fined 10s and
costs.

For many ailments it was thought that medicines had to be
given at a certain stage of the moon or they would not be effective. For example, for the bite of a mad dog (to quote Francis
Clater again):

*Take—musk, sixteen grains; native and factitious cinnabar,
of each twenty-five grains: To be given in a glass of arrack
three nights together, and the night preceeding the full of
three successive moons.*

8

Tales from the Smithy

'Go wash the smut from thy face
And come and sit at my right hand'
Old legend of King Solomon and the Temple

Blacksmiths, especially in remote villages, were called upon to
do many things besides horse-shoeing and general blacksmithing.
Haircutting and dentistry, for example. Most of them could exe-
cute a neat 'short back and sides' if called upon to do so but probably only one ever cut the hair of a king. This was Alexander
Fletcher, who worked at the Royal Smithy, Clachanturn, near
Balmoral in Scotland, where Queen Victoria's horses were shod.
The Emperor Frederick of Germany, a guest of the Queen's,
was staying at the Fife Arms Hotel, Braemar, and wanted a hair-
cut in a hurry. But no barber was available. Hearing that Alexander Fletcher was handy with the scissors he sent for him and
the job was done 'much to the Emperor's satisfaction'.

At Moelfre in Denbighshire, John Owens was widely known
as 'blacksmith and barber' and his anvil was a seat for many a
local customer.

In a Canadian paper there once appeared an advertisement

Shoeing at Lavenham, Suffolk, in the mid twentieth century. By now most blacksmiths' notices, like this one, were testifying to their wider abilities

for a blacksmith who had to be 'a good shoer, a barber and a teacher of music who can tend pianos and organs'. It was, needless to say, for a very remote community!

Dentistry done by the blacksmiths was usually very crude and people only came when their needs were extremely urgent or because they could not afford to go to a proper dentist. The customer would be held by his friends while the blacksmith seized the offending tooth with a pair of tongs and twisted it out of its socket. One blacksmith became so proud of his efforts in this line that he had a board put up in his parlour on which was written in large letters TEETH EXTRACTED—the letters being formed from extracted teeth! Some blacksmiths also did bloodletting and it is said that in parts of Scotland at one time overweight farmers would visit their blacksmith regularly to have blood taken.

Another task which the village blacksmith undertook was the

'firing' of the anvil to commemorate special occasions—which could be anything from a wedding or the opening of a village fair to a national celebration such as the relief of Mafeking or the end of World Wars I and II. In recent years it has been used at the two minutes' silence on Armistice Day. The hole in the top of the anvil is filled with gunpowder and then plugged with a block of wood. A small hole is bored in the plug and to this is laid a short train of gunpowder which is set alight by the red-hot end of a long length of iron.

Not all blacksmiths have been men. But though many wives and daughters helped their husbands or fathers in the smithy in times of illness or adversity, few women have been blacksmiths in their own right. In Chicago, however, there was a sixteen-year-old girl of whom the following was written:

> *She's a sweet little blacksmith, so limber and strong,*
> *To the blast of the bellows she carols a song;*
> *Her frock it is short, and it serves to disclose*
> *A pair of trim ankles in smart sable hose.*
> *A brown leather apron she wears over her skirt,*
> *Her cap it is crimson and blue is her shirt;*
> *With sleeve closely furled to exhibit the charm*
> *Of a biceps that pouts in a snowy white arm.*
> *So stop and regard, if you're passing the Green,*
> *This bonny young blacksmith of supple sixteen.*

At Childrey near Wantage in Berkshire in the 1920s the widow of blacksmith Walter Greenhough took over when her husband died from the kick of a horse. She had already acted as his assistant for several years and knew what it was to work hard. Of the early days she said: 'I would stand by the side of a horse ready with the pincers, hammer and nails. Bellows work, sledge work, day in, day out. Seven in the morning till five at night.'

She recalled the first time she had worked for her husband:

> *When his chance came for a forge of his own, he found*

himself stuck for a striker—for he had no money to pay for one. I said to him, 'You've always wanted to go on your own. Try me! I'm your man.' He gave a little start, flung out his right arm and with his eyes all a'glisten, said, 'Girl, you shall try your hand.' He did the smithing and me the sledging. I trembled lest I might hit his head and not the anvil the first day we worked together . . . beating out and welding a roadman's pick.

When her husband died Mrs Greenhough was determined to carry on. 'I couldn't leave the work,' she said, 'and in carrying on I had a feeling that I might be pleasing my dead man. Man and wife, smith and striker, we had fought at the forge together. And I think while I fight, he fights still. Pride . . . and love . . . at work now in the forge I always feel near to him.'

Not all blacksmiths have worked at a village smithy. Throughout blacksmith history there have been men who roamed the country helping other smiths who were behind with their work or perhaps needed a stock of shoes making up. One such was Jack Millett, better known as Pincher Jack, for his speciality was the making of tools, especially pincers, for which he had a very high reputation. His home was at Crickhowell in Wales but he travelled throughout Wales, England, Scotland and Ireland. Though he had a wife and family he only returned home every six or seven years. He had once had his own smithy and had won a championship award for horse-shoeing at an early age. But he fell on hard times, took to drink, and had to leave his shop for the road. He would call at smithies and make the tools required on the spot. He begged his clothes and slept in the poorhouse, spending what money he earned on drink. He was nearly blind. In the 1920s he charged 3s 6d for a pair of pincers which took him an hour and a half to make. He did other jobs but it was the pincers for which he was most famous—blacksmiths swore by them. He died at Crickhowell Infirmary about 1932.

Every blacksmith had his awkward horses to deal with but mules and donkeys were disliked the most for they were always

Safety first in Holland. A Dutch smith (*hoefsmid*), wearing clogs and watched by girls in local folk costume, is shoeing a wild-eyed horse in a frame. The sloping beam allows the hoof to rest at a convenient angle for the work

unpredictable. One blacksmith after a painful session of mule-shoeing penned the following lines:

In mules we find two legs behind
And two we find before;
We stand behind before we find
What the two behind be for.

At Dewsbury in Yorkshire in 1910 a crippled organ-grinder sued a blacksmith for damaging his donkey while shoeing it. He claimed that his donkey was a quiet little animal but that the blacksmith had lost his temper when the donkey had pulled away and had thrown it on the floor, kicked it twice and thrown it on the ground again. After this treatment the maltreated donkey had not been able to get up of its own accord. It had then been lifted up, said the organ-grinder, and harnessed to the barrel-organ. But still it could not move and eventually it had

had to be unharnessed, left in the blacksmith's stable and finally given away.

The organ-grinder said that the donkey was a favourite with him because it had developed a habit of braying outside certain houses 'in expectation of what it was about to receive'. His father had given £2 for it, he said. He had received another donkey from the blacksmith but this one was idle and sat down instead of working. The blacksmith, for his part, claimed that the donkey kicked itself down and that he had used the utmost care in shoeing it. The organ-grinder was eventually awarded £3 10s by the court.

Few blacksmiths would describe a horse in the words of an Indian student who wrote in 1903:

> The horse is a very noble quadruped, but when he is angry he will not do so. He is ridden on the spinal cord by the bridal and saddle. The driver places his foots on the stirrups and divides his lower limbs across the saddle and drives his animal to the meadows. He has four legs, two are on the front side and two are afterwards. These are the weapon on which he runs. He also defends himself by extending those in the rear in a parallel direction towards his foe, but this he does only when in a vexatious mood. There is no animal like the horse. No sooner they see their guardian or master, they always cry for fooding, but it is always at the morning time. They have got tail, but not so long as the cow and other such like similar animals.

Strange things seem to happen to blacksmiths. One at Kilsyth near Glasgow advertised for an assistant and was surprised several months after the position had been filled to get the following letter bearing a South African stamp:

> My Master—One day I walked in jungle, I found newspaper I take home to kraal. My mamma can read, and so can me. It say in paper because you would like blacksmith. My name not Smith, my name Kalama. If you give me job

Shoeing at Chipping Hill, near Witham, Essex in 1947, with the horse's hoof resting on the three-legged iron stand. The smithy was thought to be more than three hundred years old, but the owner (on the left) had installed electric drills and modern welding plant. When only five years old, he had been taught by his father to fashion tiny horseshoes of lead on a miniature anvil

I will change my name to make it Smith. I am also black same as you are. I am very strong, when I am sixteen I kill big, black-maned lion. I have nothing but small wife. What you command me I will do without me speak back. I have money. I come Kilsyth when you send tell me come. I will run 100 miles catch big steamer, come to you and you gif me job. I do not want money if you gif me plenty much scoff.

Now, my eternal master, I will pray to See See our great god, that you is going to send me tell come quick—

Your slave, Kalama

One blacksmith was made famous by a ghost. This man, of Lomey Town, Cradley Heath in Worcestershire, went into his smithy early one morning in 1868 and found the ashes from the fire scattered on the floor. Believing it to be the work of youths he decided to sleep in by the forge in case they came again. He awoke to see a ghostly figure in the smithy. The figure raked the red-hot ashes from the fire with its bare hands and scattered them over the floor. It then disappeared through a wall. As a result of this visitation the smithy was regarded as haunted and many local residents would never go past it at night. It was said that the air in the vicinity of the forge would suddenly become icy cold and that ghostly figures were often to be seen moving about inside the smithy.

In the same county, at Churchill near Kidderminster, was a blacksmith shop which had its forge driven by a waterwheel, a method which is thought to have been started there as far back as the thirteenth century. At Badsey, also in Worcestershire, the stone used in building the smithy came from an old abbey; it was the smiths here who made a special knife which was used by the asparagus growers of the area.

All parts of Britain have had their old and often famous blacksmith shops but they are fast disappearing. In the west country the quaint blacksmith shop at Cockington near Paignton has become a tourist centre. Though it dates probably from the fourteenth century, little is known about its origins. In 1615 a certain Anthony Hopping was a 'striker' or apprentice to the Cockington smith and eventually married his master's daughter Grace, afterwards going to Torre near Torquay. His son went to Newfoundland and was the ancestor of the Hoppings of America. Nowadays, visitors to the smithy write their names on bits of paper and stuff them into the thatch, a custom which seems to have arisen spontaneously during recent years.

At Bow in mid-Devon there stood until about 1923 a forge which had been in the hands of a family named Tozer from 1398 until 1897. The forge closed down in 1922 and was demolished the following year, being superseded by 'Tozer's' cottages built on the same site by Devon County Council.

At Broadworthy in north Devon during World War I one of the smithies was always referred to as 'The War Office' for it was said that you could always hear the latest news of activities at the front there.

The engineering firm of H. King at Sherborne in Dorset has been established over 400 years. To begin with it was a black-smith's shop and it has been handed down from father to son. In recent years it still retained a forge and two blacksmiths who did shoeing and welding though most of their work was concerned with general repairs to farm machinery, shoeing, hardening pick

An ornamental porch made at Sherborne in Dorset by one of the smiths of the engineering firm of H. King, a family concern which began as a blacksmith's shop over 400 years ago

axes, making ornamental gates and so on. In the eighteenth century one of the family, Stephen King, kept a Shop Book which is still in existence and includes such items as:

> *December 22 1788. Dressing ye ox foot 6d. Lush of Thornford.*
> *June 8 1789. Ringing 3 pigs 6d. Mrs. Oke.*
> *February 27 1790. For shoeing 2 oxen 2/-. Lord Digby.*

The blacksmith at Barrow Gurney near Bristol made thousands of mule shoes during World War I which he delivered by pony and trap to Bristol. His memory is commemorated by the iron screen which he made for Barrow Gurney church and in the iron cross of the lych gate at Kimersden.

Nether Lypratt Manor in the Cotswolds dates from 1304 but it was rebuilt by Judge Coxe in 1704. This judge employed a blacksmith to make him new entrance gates but unfortunately the blacksmith committed a serious crime and was brought for trial before the judge, who had no option but to condemn him to death. But he gave him a reprieve of two years so that he could finish the gates. The job was finished in two years to the day, the blacksmith doubtless being in no hurry to finish any earlier! The work done, he was promptly hanged.

William Allison was the blacksmith of Washington, in Durham, in 1770. At that time there was a notorious highwayman in the neighbourhood, one Robert Hazlitt, who operated mainly among the trees at the bottom of Long Bank, Wrekenton, from where he would dash out and rob the mail coaches. He wore a cloak and mask and nobody knew who he was or where he lived. But one day after a robbery a postboy saw him ride away on a fine grey horse. Not long afterwards this boy was at Washington village and saw William Allison the smith shoeing a grey horse, which the postboy was convinced was the one ridden by the highwayman. Saying nothing to anyone, the boy went off to Gateshead and told the constables what he had seen. The constables rode immediately to Washington, seized the owner of the grey horse and made him put on a mask and cloak and mount the horse. Dressed and mounted like this he was identified by several of his victims and was taken to Durham, where he confessed and was hanged. His body was removed to Wrekenton, where it was caged on a gibbet until it rotted away.

In the churchyard at Letheringsett near Holt in Norfolk is a stone to the memory of Johnson Jex, a village blacksmith who was better known for his activities as a clockmaker. He died in 1852 at the age of 73 and although, as his stone reads, he was 'born in obscurity' he advanced 'from the horseshoes to the chronometer' and acquired 'by menial labour and philosophic research' a vast and varied amount of mechanical skill and general knowledge. He was a man 'of scrupulous integrity and moral worth', but 'regardless of wealth and insensible to the voice of fame,' he lived and died a 'scientific anchorite'.

A set of shoes for the Great Exhibition of 1851 was made at Hethersett near Norwich by Mr Thrower the blacksmith, who walked all the way to London to show them. It is said that the shoes were so well made that not a hammer mark could be seen.

Further south in the village of Palgrave there used to be three smithies, the last to remain being that of the Howells, an old Palgrave family, who could trace their ancestry back over 300 years to a time when William Howell combined the duties of parish clerk and sexton with the work of a master weaver. When weaving declined in the area the Howells became carriers, and in 1847 George Howell found himself a business in sharpening the blunted picks of the navvies engaged in building the first railway in this part. From then on until recent days the Howells were blacksmiths. George's son Dennis became a qualified smith and when he died in 1931 his business had expanded to over 500 horses on the books and four assistants. In 1956 a new modern smithy was built and six men were employed—all general smiths, with three being expert farriers and one a specialist in wrought ironwork.

It was another Norfolk blacksmith—one who must remain anonymous—who sent the following bill to a customer:

	s	d
Osforarfada	2	0
Afortheos	1	0
Ashuinonim	2	0
Anafechinonimagin	1	0
	6	0

Which being translated from the Norfolk dialect reads: horse for half a day; hay for the horse; a-shoeing of him; and a-fetching of him again.

But unless he did something out of the ordinary the village blacksmith did not often get into the news. His was a quiet, honest occupation and rarely led to sensation.

Tom Teece, known as Tiny Tim, worked as a blacksmith at Crudgington in Shropshire. At nineteen he weighed eleven stone but by the time he was twenty he had reached seventeen stone; at his prime he was twenty-five stone seven pound with a waist of sixty-three inches.

Philip Parry of Marford in Flintshire celebrated his ninetieth birthday by walking into his forge to beat out the 'anvil chorus'. Among his memories were the Royal Welch Fusiliers leaving for the Crimean War and the public execution of William Jackson for the murder of his two children.

An old forge at Carlton-on-Trent in Nottinghamshire had a large brick horseshoe built into one of the walls and a notice displayed:

Gentlemen, as you pass by, upon this shoe pray cast an eye.
If it be too strait I'll make it wider, I'll ease the horse
and please the rider. If lame from shoeing as they often are,
you may have them eased with The Greatest Care.

Right: Charles Mitchell, blacksmith of Pyecombe, Sussex, in his nineties at the beginning of this century. He made hundreds of the famous Pyecombe crooks, and for thirty-five years he shod an average of 500 oxen a year, oxen being used at that time for ploughing

Below: Sean Black, present owner of Pyecombe Forge, Sussex, is an artist in metal. His work ranges from intricate metal jewellery to gates and other large pieces for Britain and America

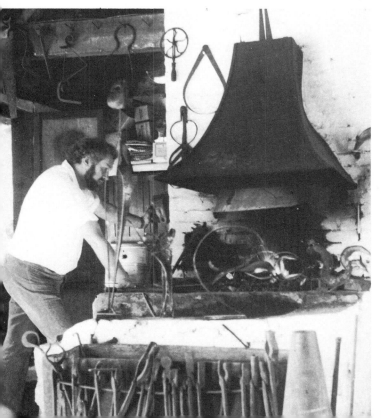

When in recent years the smithy was converted into a dwelling house the brick horseshoe and notice were retained.

Another smithy which lasted over 200 years was at Brighthelmstone near Brighton. It was famous for its ironwork as early as 1745 and at one time oxen brought the Sussex iron to the forge. And five miles inland from Brighton is a seventeenth-century smithy still famous for its traditional shepherd's crooks, which are named after the village, Pyecombe. Though the crooks are rarely used by shepherds today they are bought by bishops and others. Among purchasers in recent years have been the Archbishop of Capetown, the Bishop of Uganda and the Bishop of St Helens. The crooks used to vary with the breed of sheep they were required to catch and a typical Pyecombe crook is shaped in a curve with an opening of about one inch, just right to admit the leg bone of a Southdown sheep. The head of the crook is made of iron or steel and the haft of unpeeled hazel. Many different smiths have carried on the business at Pyecombe, one of the most famous being Barry, whose latest work was about 1855. Charles Mitchell was there for fifty-four years until 1925 and the most recent has been Sean Black, formerly of the Irish Guards, who was an artist and schoolteacher before training as a smith. His work has varied from large commissions such as the gates of the crypt of Truro Cathedral and various pieces for American customers to intricate metal jewellery.

The Mortimers of Sunnyhill in Berkshire had a long career as general smiths. They shod horses for Queen Anne, did work occasionally for Queen Victoria and King Edward VII (when Prince of Wales) and were the official locksmiths for keeping the locks and keys of Windsor Park gates in order.

At the death in 1789 of William Perrott the blacksmith of Frilsham in Berkshire the following epitaph was written:

Good ale and beer he loved exceeding well,
And while in health of both he took his fill;
But no-one grieve too much within their mind—
Although he has gone he has left some beer behind.

The Pearces of Eardiston in Shropshire operated for over 250 years in the same village and before that, probably from medieval times, the family had been carrying on the same trade in the village of Rodington near Wellington. In recent years a member of the family, J. M. Pearce, took up ornamental ironwork and was responsible for the War Memorial gates at Holy Trinity church, Oswestry and many other such jobs.

At Disley near Stockport the Rowbothams started black-smithing in the early seventeenth century. The smithy stood under a pear tree. John Rowbotham, who was working there until the end of the 1930s, recalled having to stand on a box to reach the anvil when he started work at the age of seven, but he developed into a brawny man weighing sixteen stone. He was smith to Lord Newton of Lymme Hall and later to the Hon R. W. D. Legh, and he had a reputation as a man who had never come off the worse in his handling of horses. He only took one holiday, which was to the Isle of Man. He never shaved, and in the early days he reckoned to have a glass of beer for every horse he shod, but in his old age he changed this to four pints of milk a day. He was a non-smoker and his recipe for long life was: 'Go to bed early, rise early, have a joke often, do a good turn often and you'll live as long as you like.'

The smithy at Chipping Hill near Witham in Essex is known to be over 300 years old and a forge of some kind probably existed there for centuries before that. At Harrold in Berkshire the blacksmith at one time 'rang' pigs with rings made from old horse-nails; he used to go round the village fitting the rings at a penny ha'penny a time.

The firm of Charles Burrell of Thetford in Suffolk stems from a master smith Joseph Burrell of 1770 and there had been a smith there for many years before that. At another smithy in Thetford which existed in the eighteenth century near the Fleece Tavern the famous Coke of Holkham used to hold his early 'sheepshearing and agricultural' meetings.

The village blacksmith was a man of great consequence in the

A modern smith, C. J. Benson, in an old-fashioned smithy near Ambleside in the Lake District

community and was usually regarded as next in importance to the squire and parson. In a Scottish parish a young new minister was anxious to find out how he stood with his parishioners. He put out feelers to a local farmer who replied, 'Weel, Sir, if ye hear nae complaints, dinna seek ony. If we get a guid smith and on honest miller, we can mak' do wi' a gie ordinary minister.'

But that was in the good old days for the blacksmith. As he moved into the twentieth century he was to feel less wanted and to face many a problem and many a crisis.

9

The End of the Road

'The blacksmith's shop is vacant now,
Weeds grow round the door'
American Ironsmith

The life of a village blacksmith has never been an easy one
and he has rarely been able to acquire any substantial wealth.
It is difficult to compare early prices and wages with those of
later times. One of the earliest records is dated AD 843 when 2s
was charged for four shoes and nails in Wales. In the same
century the tools of one smith were estimated to be worth 10s:
a large anvil 5s, bellows 8d and pincers, sledge, paring knife and
rasp 4d each.

In the time of Elizabeth I the wages of a blacksmith in
Chester were 2d to 2½d a day without meat and drink, or 6d
to 7d with drink but not meat. In 1614 the accounts of Robert
Loder, a farmer at Harwell in Berkshire included one to the
local smith John Poulton.

Imprimis
Paid him for shoeing my five horses and a
gelding   *19s   4d*

*Item for work done about by plough and
pointing shares and coulters etc*   *18s 1d*
*Item for odd works as cart cloutes, for a
thing to cut want hills 2/4, for hatchets etc*   *16s 4d*

This smith, like many a smith before and after him, was in debt when he died. Among his creditors were Robert Church a Thames bargeman (for a chaldron of sea-coal), Jacob an ironmonger (for iron), a linen draper, a woollen draper and a tailor. The creditors took an inventory of the blacksmith's goods, including the stocks of iron left in the smithy, the bellows, the anvil and all his tools. But altogether they were only valued at seven pounds.

John Dale, a Cheshire blacksmith, sent this account to a customer in 1780:

Charles Lees bill Depter to John and William Dale

		s	d
January 1st	*Left Unpaid of the last bill*	1	5
Jan 12-13	*2 Shoes and 10 removes all steelt at tos and heels*	2	11
Jan 18	*an axe ground and a halm for it and a hook*	2	3
Feb 18	*2 Sole plates for a ploo 7 pound*	2	4
March 23	*A new spade*	4	6
April 17	*4 Shoes barefut and 1 remove*	1	6
,, ,,	*4 removes and Salve and Oils for a Mares foot*		7

The blacksmith often exchanged goods and services with other tradesmen in lieu of receiving cash, and some accounts went on for year after year without being settled. The butcher paid his shoeing bill with meat, the baker with bread, while the carpenter relied on repairs and decorating of the blacksmith's house to meet his bills. Small farmers would pay partly in rabbits or perhaps the occasional pheasant. One mid-nineteenth-century man provided four loads of manure and a day's work at the smithy in return for having his family's clogs 'ironed', while another allowed the blacksmith's sow to visit his boar in return for some shoeing.

An account book, 1848-54, of the village blacksmith at Harwarden (where Gladstone lived) included:

3 removes, 2 shoes	*6s*	
New head to turnip how		*6d*
3 new hoops to barrow wheels	*1s*	
Hooping pair of carriage wheels	*1s*	*6d*
2 timber dogs		*4d*
Frost nailing one horse		*6d*
Laying pair of plow irons	*2s*	*3d*

At the end of the nineteenth century wages and prices were still very low, but they varied with the district. In the large towns where the blacksmiths had become organised the prices

Blacksmith and striker at work in a modern forge

were just about high enough to give them a living, but in many country places they were pathetically low. At a time when it cost 7s to have a horse shod in one of the large towns it was possible to get it done in out-of-the-way places for 2s, or even less if the customer haggled. A town blacksmith who visited the West Country in 1899 wrote to the editor of his trade journal:

> I dare not think what you and my brother farriers will say and think of the West of England farriers shoeing at 2s a set. But, Sir, this is not the worst. There are some shoeing for 1s 8d and I am told that you can get a horse shod on the borders of Devon and Somerset for 1s 6d per set. I say such men ought to be drummed out of the trade—stone-breaking on the road is good enough for them.

Three years later the editor of the same journal was writing:

> It is a crying shame and a disgrace that it should be possible for men to be found who undertake shoeing a cart-horse for 3s 6d, because all who know the trade are aware that it can only be done at a loss and no man can live on a loss.

The cost of the raw materials—iron and coal—increased until by the middle of the nineteenth century it was no longer economical to make horseshoes by hand in any quantity. In 1858 A. V Newton of Chancery Lane patented a machine to make horseshoes and after that several patents were taken out, but apparently with little or no success until in 1878 a machine for making horseshoes was brought to England from America by a Mr Seeling, who started The Horse Shoe Manufacturing Co at Cubitt Town, East London, and later expanded to Germany and Austria. In 1883 this company amalgamated with the Globe Horse Nail Co to become The United Horse Shoe and Nail Co, with Thomas D. Richardson in charge.

The United Horse Shoe and Nail went bankrupt and the business was sold to the British and Colonial Horse Shoe and

THE BRITISH AND COLONIAL
HORSE SHOE & MACHINE COMPANY,
LIMITED.
The only Makers of Richardson's Patents,
AND
Improved Horse, Mule, and Pony Shoes.

*Our improved facilities of production enable us to make
the cheapest and best in the world.*

SINGLE FULLER, DOUBLE FULLER, & PLAIN SHOES
MADE FROM THE BEST IRON OR STEEL.
Plain and Fullered Bars a Speciality.

Our Shoes have met with special favour from the practical Horse Shoers throughout Great Britain and the Colonies. It is our aim to produce a style of Shoes which are suited to the wants of the Horse Shoer, by their cheapness in price to save him money, by their regularity and eveness of shape and finish to save him time in fitting out, and by having sufficient wear to give satisfaction to his customers.

*Contractors to many of the principal Tramway & Omnibus Companies
Quotations to Specifications.*

NELSON WHARF, MILLWALL,
LONDON, E.
AND AT
GLOBE IRON WORKS,
WALSALL, STAFFS.
T. D. RICHARDSON, Managing Director.

Early twentieth-century notice of the largest horseshoe manufacturer in Europe

Machine Co of London and Walsall. The British and Colonial became the largest horseshoe manufacturers in Europe, at one period making over 750 different kinds of shoes, which were sent all over the world.

The nails for the horseshoes were still being hand-made in small quantities at the outbreak of World War I. In the Black Country of Staffordshire, around Wigan and Birmingham, it had been a cottage industry for over 600 years. The small houses of the nailmakers had smithies attached to them. Before the American War of Independence nails were sent to America. Wages were low and even the children had to be put to work at the earliest possible age to augment the family income.

These old nailmakers made a surprising number of different types of nail and each had its own name, such as sixpenny, ten-penny, or fourpenny, which had nothing to do with their price but had developed out of the practice of taking the weight of 1,000 nails which could amount to six pounds or ten pounds etc.

At the zenith of the home-made nail industry about 50,000 people were employed in the Black Country alone. Orrell, near Wigan, was the last centre to survive and one Edward Hall is thought to have been the last nailmaker.

Machine-made nails were available from Germany as early as 1883 but they 'only stood three twists in a vice', and it was said that during the Boer War when the British cavalry were shod with these German nails many disasters befell the horses, whereas De Witt's horses, which were shod with nails made by hand from Swedish iron, avoided them.

The Englishman Capewell who migrated to America became famous for horseshoe nails, inventing machinery and forming a company for making them. In 1889 he returned to England and founded works at Millwall, which later were moved to Hadley in Shropshire. A factory was added in Canada. Another well-known name was the Norwegian firm of Mustad, which opened a factory in Bristol and at one time manufactured nails in nine different countries.

About the same time as machine-made nails came machine-made coke 'breeze', which did away with the need for the blacksmith to wash his own coke.

By the beginning of the twentieth century, after the years of agricultural depression, the village blacksmith began to come into his own again and business started to improve.

Then came the motor car.

It took quite a while for the blacksmith to realise that the motor age would affect his trade, and many more years for him to understand that his old way of life was disappearing for ever. The editor of a British trade paper could write in 1903:

> According to reports from all parts of the country the motor craze is bearing its fruit in bringing the machine into contempt. Contempt is scarcely the word—most people are simply disgusted with the craze. The novelty will soon wear off, like the brilliancy of tinsel or cheap jewellery. And then it will be relegated to the limbo of exploded fads.

And, three years later, an American blacksmiths' journal commented on whether the car would ever replace the horse:

> I cannot see it and think that those who look at it in that way are short-sighted. Twenty years from now the junk dealers will be buying up all the old automobiles for scrap. It will be just like the bicycles—going out about as quickly. The man who believes that the automobile is going to supplant the horse in his use is to my mind completely in the dark.

The blacksmiths did what they could to hold up the motor age but they must have soon realised that they were fighting a losing battle. When the Duke of Beaufort used a car in Gloucestershire to travel to the hunt, the blacksmiths reminded him that other masters of hounds had requested their followers not to use such a vehicle. But the Duke explained that he was not using a car to do away with horses but solely to save time in getting to the meet, the car enabling him to leave home three-quarters of an hour later than if he went in a horse and trap.

When the first cars banged and spluttered their way through the village streets the blacksmith tended to look on them with disdain, but at the same time he regarded himself as an expert when they went wrong and were brought to him for repair. But some of the wise blacksmiths realised that here was the future for them and acted accordingly. In 1911 one of them, Stan Merritt, wrote some lines in the manner of Longfellow's *The Village Blacksmith*:

Beneath a huge electric sign,
The village smith now sits;
His brawny form, though plump and fat,
His easy chair just fits.

The old clay pipe is laid away,
His brow reveals no sweat;
He calmly views the cars roll up
And puffs a cigarette.

Six shining pumps adorn the spot
Where once the anvil stood:
The heavy traffic daily pays
This modern Robin Hood.

The invasion of the motor car was halted when war was declared in 1914.

Since the first days when horses were used in battle, wars have generally meant more business for the blacksmith. As *Punch* put it in 1866, in a little poem entitled 'The War Blacksmith':

So Vulcan all his toil and stock
Must on War's tasks bestow,
And iron, good for spade and share,
For sword and gun must go.

Horse-Shoes for the War.

To Shoeing-Smiths of the United Kingdom North of London.

Will all Smiths who can supply small or large quantities of Horse-Shoes to pattern apply AT ONCE to W. Jones Anstey, 33 Gledhow Avenue, Roundhay, Leeds, the Inspector under the War Office for the same, who will send full *particulars of what is required.*

All payments will be made weekly direct from the War Office.

GOD SAVE THE KING.

Advertisement issued near the beginning of World War I

If the blacksmith went to war, he was as a rule rarely involved in the actual fighting. But during the American War of Independence the 19th Light Dragoons, an English regiment, were covering a retreat closely followed by a large body of American cavalry. A Yorkshire farrier with the British was in charge of a portable forge, and as the Americans approached he suddenly wheeled it round and pointed the tube of the bellows at them. Thinking it was a cannon the American cavalry drew reign and the Dragoons were able to effect a safe retreat, for which the blacksmith received much praise.

When World War I broke out in 1914 a large number of horses was immediately commandeered for the forces and this reduced the amount of trade for the farriers. But this was evened out by the enlistment of the younger men. The supply of machine-made horseshoes was not enough; the older men at home were needed to make more and advertisements began to appear asking for large quantities of shoes. In September 1914 there appeared the one reproduced on the opposite page.

Soon over ten tons of horseshoes a week were arriving at Woolwich Arsenal alone. But though the blacksmiths were more than willing to do their bit for the war, costs of iron and labour rose so much that they began to find it difficult to make a living. By December 1914 the cost of making a shoe was more than the War Office would offer and the blacksmiths' representative for the war effort, W. Jones Anstey, severed his connection with the War Office.

In the north of England where the blacksmiths were asked to produce fifty tons of shoes a week, a meeting of master farriers sent a deputation to Lord Kitchener asking for more money and for the re-establishment of Jones Anstey. A curt reply from the Secretary to the War Office stated:

I am commanded by the Army Council to inform you that the facts put forward by you in regard to the supply of Army Horse Shoes by Farriers has been fully considered,

*but it is regretted that your request for an increased
price ... cannot be complied with.*

Meanwhile the poor horses were experiencing conditions worse
than had even been known in previous wars. At the same time,
with many of the younger blacksmiths enlisted and quite a few
of the older ones working at army camps where they could earn
much more money than in their own smithies, the quality of the
general work deteriorated and there were complaints from the
Front about the poor quality of the shoes sent. In April 1915
Woolwich Arsenal announced that they would buy no more
hand-made shoes from British blacksmiths but instead would
obtain machine-made shoes from America.

From that time on the British horses were all shod with
machine-made shoes from America. Yet by one of those strange
arrangements that happen in war, the horses of the Allied forces
fighting with the British were shod by British blacksmiths. And
this was no small business, for by July 1915 America had shipped
80,000 horses to Europe.

But all in all, though it meant very hard work at times, most
of the blacksmiths were able to earn enough money to put
aside some which they were to need in the years to follow. Now
more than ever, the motor began to take over—a change that
was expedited by the wastage of horses. More and more the
notice 'Motors mended' began to appear beside the sign 'Horses
shod', and one enterprising blacksmith near London, having
been called out to repair an aeroplane that had crash-landed
nearby, added 'Aeroplanes mended' as well.

For a while after the war, war-surplus shoes were available
in heavy quantities, and in 1920 a London firm was still able
to offer '2,000,000 horse and mule shoes for sale—all government surplus', and also 'Bayonets (English) for toeing knives,
6s a dozen.'

Too much had happened for things ever to be the same again
and, overall, it was a losing battle for the blacksmiths, particularly during the depressed period of the 1930s. The years

The increase in horse-riding for pleasure gives work to some blacksmiths, like this smith of Port St Mary in the Isle of Man

between the two world wars saw many of them go out of business. It needed a great effort on the part ot the village smith to adapt himself to the new circumstances. He had to understand that the day of the horse as a transport animal, apart from riding for pleasure, was over; he also had to realise that the implements and machines used in agriculture were becoming far more complicated and that if he was still to repair them he had to learn something about engineering.

For those who remained in the business and were able to adapt, the new work brought its compensations. One blessing, especially for the older blacksmith, was the disappearance of the heavy cart-horse, for shoeing these heavy horses had brought the active life of many a blacksmith to a premature end.

Those who held on saw things gradually swing round a little. Helped by the various organisations they trained to meet the new needs of the countryside, learning welding, accountancy, mechanics, the art of making decorative ironwork and so forth.

Farm horses decreased rapidly but farm implements still broke down or wore out and needed mending, while racing stables continued to provide some custom. And as the years went by there was a renewal of interest in the horse in pony and riding clubs, while hunting, racing and show jumping became more popular than ever.

The blacksmith changed over to electric light and had the telephone installed. He found that his new customers could not afford the time to send their horses to the forge so he bought himself a van or motor-cycle and took his forge to the farms and stables. But despite all this, the old forges one by one closed down in the countryside and many a blacksmith said his sad farewells.

The same thing was happening in America and most other industrial countries. From the *American Ironsmith* in December 1937 came:

Under the spreading chestnut tree
A hallowed relic stands,

A mobile blacksmith, Joseph Marshall of Sheldon, Birmingham, takes his anvil and tools on his motor-cycle and tours farms and riding schools in the district

The village shop is a memory
Like the old smith's sinewy hands.

The blacksmith's shop is vacant now,
Weeds grow round the door,
We see no waggon there or plow,
Nor hear the bellows roar.

But it was not all gloom and nostalgia. Many of the younger smiths were fighting back. Farrier, smith, engineer, welder, artist—this was the modern village blacksmith. Basically he remains the same honest and respected man whom Longfellow wrote of, and now, with his new skills, he can take on a fresh role in this technological age. The village blacksmith may never be the same again, but the smith will surely go on as long as iron needs to be forged in this world.

APPENDIX

The Village Blacksmith

written in 1810 by Henry Wadsworth Longfellow

Under a spreading chestnut-tree
   The village smithy stands;
The smith, a mighty man is he,
   With large and sinewy hands;
And the muscles of his brawny arms
   Are strong as iron bands.

His hair is crisp, and black, and long;
   His face is like the tan;
His brow is wet with honest sweat,
   He earns whate'er he can,
And looks the whole world in the face,
   For he owes not any man.

Week in, week out, from morn till night,
   You can hear his bellows blow;
You can hear him swing his heavy sledge,
   With measured beat and slow,
Like a sexton ringing the village bell,
   When the evening sun is low.

And children coming home from school
   Look in at the open door;
They love to see the flaming forge,
   And hear the bellows roar,
And catch the burning sparks that fly
   Like chaff from a threshing-floor.

He goes on Sunday to the church,
   And sits among his boys;
He hears the parson pray and preach,
   He hears his daughter's voice
Singing in the village choir,
   And it makes his heart rejoice.

It sounds to him like her mother's voice
   Singing in Paradise!
He needs must think of her once more,
   How in the grave she lies;
And with his hard, rough hand he wipes
   A tear out of his eyes.

Toiling,—rejoicing,—sorrowing,
   Onward through life he goes;
Each morning sees some task begin,
   Each evening sees it close;
Something attempted, something done,
   Has earned a night's repose.

Thanks, thanks to thee, my worthy friend,
   For the lesson thou has taught!
Thus at the flaming forge of life
   Our fortunes must be wrought;
Thus, on its sounding anvil shaped
   Each burning deed and thought.

Bibliography

Adam, Arthur *The History of the Worshipful Company of Blacksmiths* 1951

Allen, Matthew *The Farrier's Assistant* 1737

Arnold, James *The Shell Book of Country Crafts* 1968

Blacksmiths Company Exhibition Catalogue 1894

Blacksmith's Craft, The Council for Small Industries in Rural Areas 5th Imp 1968

Booth, Charles *Life and Labour of the People in London* 1903

Burdon, W. *The Gentleman's Pocket-Farrier* 1730

Burritt, Elihu *Why I left the Anvil and other Papers* 1879

Carley, Gaius *Memoirs* Edited F. W. Steer 1963

Cathcart, W. H. *The Value of Science in the Smithy and Forge* 1916

Central Youth Employment Executive *Agricultural Mechanic and the Blacksmith* 1969

Clater, Francis *Everyman his own Farrier* 1810

Coulson, J. (Ed) *The Saints* 1958

Curti, Merle *The Learned Blacksmith* 1937

Derrick, F. *Country Craftsmen* 1945

Derry, T. K. and Williams, T. I. *A Short History of Technology* 1960

Dunlop and Ranken Iron and Steel Catalogue
English Farrier, The 1636
Evans, Ewart *The Horse in the Furrow* 1960
Everett, James *The Village Blacksmith (Samuel Hick)* 1845
Farrier and Naturalist Volumes 1-3 1828-30
Farriery Rural Industries Bureau 1955
Fleming, George *Horse-Shoes and Horse-Shoeing* 1869
Gent, R. W. *The Experienced Farrier* 1720
Griffiths, William *Practical Treatise on Farriery* 1784
Guide to Gretna Green Marrying Establishments 1823
Hampshire Field Club, Papers of Vol 8
Hennell, T. *The Countryman at Work* 1947
Hick, Samuel *Entire Sanctification* 1831
Hogg, Garry *Hammer and Tongs* 1964
Holmes, C. M. *The Principles and Practice of Horse-Shoeing* 1930
Hone's Everyday Book 1830
Kelly, Thomas *Gretna Green: or the Elopement of Miss D.* 1823
Lawrence, R. M. *The Magic of the Horse-Shoe* 1898
Lillico, J. W. *Blacksmith's Manual Illustrated* 1930
Maitland, S. R. *The Dark Ages* 1899
McDougall, R. *The Gretna Blacksmith's Story* 1928
Moore, Thomas *Handbook of Practical Smithing and Forging* 1941
National Registration of Farriers 1902
New Survey of London Life and Labour Vol 2 1931
Niall, I. *Country Blacksmith* 1966
Richardson, C. *Practical Farriery* 1950
Robins, F. W. *The Smith* 1953
Roaring Blacksmith's Resolution, The 1858
Robson, L. C. F. *The Farriers of London* 1949
Smith, M. C. ('Claverhouse') *Irregular Border Marriages* 1934
Stevenson, J. A. R. *The Din of a Smithy* 1932
Stowe, E. J. *Crafts of the Countryside* 1948
Trew, C. G. *The Horse through the Ages* 1953

Ward, Gordon R. *On Dating Old Horse-Shoes* 1939
Waylem, James *A History . . . of the town of Marlborough* 1854
Wymer, Norman *English Country Crafts* 1946

Acknowledgements

Many of the short extracts and stories in the book have been taken from the *Farriers Journal*, a publication which has represented the blacksmiths since 1894. I would like to thank the proprietors and the editor for their kind permission to quote from the interesting material they have published over the years.

I should also like to make acknowledgement to the many organisations that have helped me in my search for information. They include the Council for Small Industries in Rural Areas, the Museum of English Rural Life, the British Museum (Department of Printed Books and Department of Manuscripts), the Worshipful Company of Farriers, the Worshipful Company of Blacksmiths, the National Library of Wales, the National Library of Scotland, Cambridge (Massachusetts) Public Library, and public libraries—especially the local history departments—in many parts of Britain.

R.W.

Index

Illustrations are indicated by italic figures